A GALLERY OF NEW TESTAMENT ROGUES

D1557017

A GALLERY
OF
NEW TESTAMENT
ROGUES

From Herod to Satan

by
JOHN R. BODO

THE WESTMINSTER PRESS
Philadelphia

Copyright © 1979 The Westminster Press

Scripture quotations from the Revised Standard
Version of the Bible are copyrighted 1946, 1952,
© 1971, 1973 by the Division of Christian Education of the National Council of the Churches of
Christ in the U.S.A., and are used by permission.

BOOK DESIGN BY DOROTHY ALDEN SMITH

First edition

Published by The Westminster Press ®
Philadelphia, Pennsylvania

PRINTED IN THE UNITED STATES OF AMERICA

9 8 7 6 5 4 3 2 1

Library of Congress Cataloging in Publication Data

Bodo, John R
A gallery of New Testament rogues.

1. Bible. N.T.—Biography. 2. Rogues and
vagabonds—Biography. I. Title.
BS2448.R63B63   225.9′22 [B]   78-13984
ISBN 0-664-24227-8

Contents

Preface

The greatest handicap from which Biblical characters suffer is that they are in the Bible. It is hard enough to enter the world of the Bible, so remote from us in time and culture. It is twice as hard to bring to life the men and women of the New Testament from the embalmed state to which we have allowed their "sacredness" to condemn them.

While we consider the Old Testament as much a part of God's Word as the New, we treat Old Testament characters with greater realism because, after all, they are "pre-Jesus." We do not feel compelled to whitewash Jacob but let him be what he was—both crook and man of God. Nor are we unduly disturbed to catch David, the great poet-king, in treachery and adultery. In my earlier book, *Adam and Eve and You, A Genesis Family Album,* I have felt free to deal with the patriarchs in a rather human way.

But we have tended to type New Testament characters according to their most obvious traits, burying their individuality, their richness, their complexity. We have dealt worst with those we have meant to honor most—the "saints." Few of us ever penetrate beyond the "too-good-to-be-true" stereotypes in which we hold captive such complicated, juicily human personalities as "Saint" John the Baptist or "Saint" Peter or "Saint" Paul.

There are other New Testament characters who appear as villains in the story and whom we have accordingly embalmed in equally boring stereotypes of villainy. Names like Herod or Judas or Pilate are seldom more than signals at which to hiss and boo. By writing them off uncritically as "too bad to be true," we deprive ourselves of the company of some complex, fascinating, individual human beings who might have been "saints " had they been differently cast.

In *A Gallery of New Testament Rogues,* I follow my conviction (shared by "Saint" Paul!) that "saint" and "sinner" are virtually synonymous. The Bible, for me, is the record of the acts of *God. He* is sacred—and he alone. But he works and reveals himself through characters as mixed up as we are, living lives as confused as ours. That is what makes these characters inexhaustibly interesting and relevant: that they are so much like us and, at the same time, actors in God's Word, usually unwitting, often witless, always undeserving of God's love—just like you and me.

Yes, the New Testament is different from the Old because of the presence of Jesus, the God-Man, just as the world has been—and ever will be—different for his presence. The stories and character sketches of these "rogues," these saintly sinners and sinful saints, all reflect the impact of his life and ministry, his death and victory, upon them. But my main purpose has been to de-embalm them, bring them back to life from the torpor of our "too good to be true" and "too bad to be true" stereotypes of them, let them become a living part of God's word to us, not in spite of but because of their haunting likeness to us.

I dedicate this little book to Dr. John Alexander Mackay, President Emeritus of Princeton Theological Seminary, whose richly poetic vision of "the life of man in the light of God," coupled with his personal generosity to me, has been a treasured source of light for my life.

1

HEROD THE GREAT
King of Christmas Fame

Matthew 2

The Gospels present not just two but three Christmas parties given in honor of the little boy after whom Christmas was named. Two of these parties we love to remember in drama and song. We join the Shepherds' party, sharing their speechless adoration. We take our places with the Wise Men, offering our gifts to the Christ child. Year after year, the memory of these two parties fills us with wonder and thanksgiving.

But there was a third party occasioned by the Savior's birth. It is seldom remembered because it does not fit into the mood of Christmas. It is too incongruous, too horrible, too futile. We would rather not think about King Herod's Christmas party. We would rather pretend that it has no significance for us.

There were not too many small children in Bethlehem when Herod's soldiers descended on the town, but in their innocent death they raised a cry that all our carols have not been able to drown. What should we do about Herod's

Christmas party? How can we fit it into the meaning and message of Christmas?

Matthew's Interpretation

The massacre of the children is reported only by Matthew, and it is obvious that he himself was perplexed as to what to do with the story. He, too, would have preferred to skip it, to pretend that it did not happen. But believing that it could not have happened against God's wishes, or even without some purpose on God's part, Matthew tried to discover that purpose. His explanation is plodding and poetic, ingenious and farfetched, naïve and inspired.

Matthew uses the story to glorify God for miraculously saving and protecting Jesus. Warned by God's messenger, the holy family flees to Egypt where so many thousands of Jews had found refuge in the course of their country's troubled history. Then, when the Savior returns from Egypt, Matthew is reminded of Moses, under whose leadership God had delivered his people hundreds of years earlier. Against this background of sacred history, the story becomes a symbol of both providence and deliverance.

The story has not always been as studiously ignored as it is today. During the Middle Ages, when Christian piety was more earthy and less squeamish, the massacre of the Holy Innocents was a frequent theme. Instead of being shocked into silence, Christian writers and artists saw in these murdered infants the first martyrs of the faith. Did they not, in a very deep sense, give their lives for the Lord? We have a more recent echo of this piety in Holman Hunt's painting, "Triumph of the Innocents," in which the infants, awakened from their brief sleep, are dancing on the banks of the river of life, singing the praises of the Lord.

All these interpretations of the story are suggestive and spiritually enriching, but they do not do justice to the central figure who is as much a part of Christmas as the shepherds and the Wise Men. Herod, in fact, is a more plausible, more universal figure than either the shepherds or the Wise Men. The shepherds are minority representatives. They represent that minority of simple folk whose simplicity is not ignorance but innocence, and whose religion is not superstition but intuitive communion with God. The Wise Men are also minority representatives. They represent that minority of the world's great men who can afford to be humble because they know enough to know how little they really know.

Herod is different. He is the representative of the majority. He is our brother.

Herod the Man

At first blush, we feel little kinship with a petty tyrant of two thousand years ago. It seems farfetched and outrageous to be compared with a man who murdered his wife and three of his sons as well as all the rivals, real or imaginary, who ever came within the orbit of his savage, suspicious nature. It seems ridiculous to be mentioned in the same breath with a cold-blooded murderer of children, when we yearly delight our own children and the children of loved ones and friends with Christmas gifts and Christmas fun.

But Herod has been somewhat misrepresented, because we see him in the mirror of Christian tradition. By judging him solely on the basis of the Gospel record, we come up with a monster, subhuman and unreal. For a more human view of Herod, we have to consult non-Christian sources, which do exist. From these sources, Herod emerges every bit as cruel as we have come to know him, but with his cruelty revealed as a part of cruel times and crude standards rather than as a result of any unique or special perversity.

No Stranger to Greatness

Herod lived at a time when his cruelty was not even conspicuous. The story of his dynasty reads like the story of the House of Borgia. It is a story of treachery, deceit, and blood. But such were the instruments of power in those dark days—and are they really any different in our enlightened day? At least in those days murder always bore a personal stamp and involved personal risk. Anonymous, impersonal, CIA-style killing did not appear until our civilized, modern times!

Judged by the standards of his own time, then, Herod appears as a ruthless, able, and relatively successful ruler. He foisted himself on the Jewish people who despised him because he was a foreigner. But he managed to keep a measure of peace in their war-racked country and even to enlarge the country's borders. He played politics with the Romans, who also despised him because he was an underling. But he managed to die a natural death—which was more than most of Rome's puppets were able to do. He was given the title of "the Great" and, upon closer scrutiny, it appears that he was no stranger to greatness.

From the Gospel narrative it is hard to see any great-

ness in Herod. Richard Crashaw, the seventeenth-century
English poet, speaks of him with mingled horror and pity:

> Why art thou troubled, Herod? What
>   vain fear,
> Thy blood-revolving breast to rage
>   doth move?
> Heaven's King, who doffs himself weak
>   flesh to wear,
> Comes not to rule in wrath, but serve
>   in love;
> Nor would he this thy feared crown
>   from thee tear,
> But give thee a better with himself
>   above.
> Poor jealousy! Why should he wish to
>   prey
> Upon thy crown, who gives his own
>   away?

It is hard to see anything in Herod's slaughter of the
infants except the ghastly fear and rage of a frustrated old
man. What danger could come to Herod from a newborn
child at this point, when Herod would surely be dead long
before the child had a chance to grow to manhood? Why
should Herod unleash such violence against this child
whose mission to the world, according to prophecy, was
to be a mission of peace?

But look at it this way. Suppose that Herod, instead
of being merely impotent and irrational, was actually far
more perceptive than we give him credit for being? The
Gospels tell us that the demons recognized Jesus as the
Messiah before even his disciples were certain of his identity! The soul of Herod was the headquarters of many
demons, many insightful demons. Herod was "diaboli-

cally" clever in many of his political and military decisions. Might not these same "demons" give him a correct
intuition concerning the real significance of this baby?

A Unique Tribute

This much can be said for Herod: he took Jesus seriously. He knew that if Jesus was allowed to live and to
fulfill his mission, it would be a deathblow for Herod and
the likes of him. Herod sensed that the threat of this
nonviolent Messiah who was coming into the world as a
little child was the greatest threat he had ever faced. For
violence can always be held in check or defeated by
greater violence, but against moral and spiritual power
violence is powerless.

In this perspective, then, Herod fittingly supplements
the homage paid to Jesus by the shepherds and the Wise
Men. The shepherds saw in the Christ child the sign of
God's mercy and love. The Wise Men found in him the
token of God's fathomless wisdom. Herod failed to see
these things, but he sensed just as surely another, equally
important reality: he sensed, in the advent of the Christ,
the justice and the inevitable judgment of God.

The massacre of the infants was as truly an act of
homage as the shepherds' adoration or the Wise Men's
costly gifts. In fact, it was the most startling, the most
discerning homage Christ received during his lifetime—
until Caiaphas and Pilate awarded him the cross.

The Herod in Us

But what do we have in common with Herod?
On the surface, very little. All the instincts and im-

pulses to which this ancient Oriental despot was able to give free rein have been domesticated in our "civilized" way of life and, in times of peace at least, are being held in check. However, all these instincts and impulses are alive and operating in all of us—and in each of us.

Herod's insecurity is our insecurity—a grotesquely distorted but recognizable image of our insecurity. A two-year-old boy pinching his baby sister viciously is showing a bit of Herod's jealousy. Herod's spirit is at work in the pretty mother whose heart suddenly grows cold because her daughter looks just a shade too mature, too striking, in that new dress. Herod's murderous impulses are being sublimated in the daily routine of a bureaucrat who deliberately fails to help an associate, in order to keep him at bay as a potential rival. Think of all the mean little things we do because of our fear of rivals: in the family, in our life at work, in our social life. Shades of Herod!

Herod's evil mind is a mirror of our minds. The image it throws at us is exaggerated, no doubt, but it is clearly recognizable. Herod was unable to believe that anyone's motives could be gracious because his own motives were so mixed and foul. Herod was treacherous, so he expected only treachery. He was greedy, so he looked for greed in everyone. He was confused and annoyed by the very appearance of goodness, because he did not know how to cope with goodness.

Someone says an unusually friendly "Good morning!" to us and we wonder, "What does he want?" Someone makes a generous gift to a good cause and we wonder, "Is he after some business or is it just for prestige?" Our friends bid us good night after a nice party and we wonder, "How many of these friends would ever look me up

or do anything to help me, if suddenly I lost everything?"
Shades of Herod!

Herod's love of force is also a present fact in our
hearts. Herod the Great is dead. The Roman Empire is
dust. In our own day, Hitler and Mussolini did their dirty
work and passed on. The saying of Jesus, "All who take
the sword will perish by the sword," has proved to be true
ten thousand times. Still we do not learn. Still we fight—
and even win—wars, but are unable to make a lasting
peace because we do not trust the weapons of peace. We
only trust the weapons of war. We raise billions for arms
and give away a few skimpy millions for hunger relief and
technical assistance overseas, while condemning our own
educational, cultural, and welfare systems to undignified,
and often fruitless, begging. Shades of Herod!

No, we do not put babies to the sword these days: we
napalm them; at least we did until we were forced to stop
that madness—in humiliating defeat. That was yesterday.
But if the bomb rattlers among us have their way, it might
start again tomorrow. Nor will it ever end until we begin
to believe, really believe, that peace cannot be secured by
war, and that what Jesus said about the other cheek and
the second mile was not pious tommyrot but the spiritual
foundation of the only workable program for peace.

Meanwhile, the record of Herod's Christmas party
remains as an everlasting reminder of the futility of evil
and the sure triumph of God. As Herod the Great was
unable to murder the Christ child, so are we unable to halt
the march of the Prince of Peace. Whether we oppose him
by active, violent means or, just as meanly, by lip service
and an unholy effort to make him serve our ends, he
always slips away from us. And his cause, God's own
cause of justice and peace, goes marching on.

2

JOHN THE BAPTIST
He Said He Was Ready to Retire

Mark 1:1–8; John 1:29–34; Luke 7:18–28

Retirement affects people in a variety of ways. Gail Sheehy, in her book *Passages,* tells about a man named Tyler who had gone into advertising when he really wanted to be a writer. The compromise depressed him even though he was successful. But he did not allow his success to spoil his boyhood dream. Rather, he began to prepare, carefully, methodically, for the day when he would step down from his agency post and devote himself to his real calling. It was not easy. Much of the time, while moving up in the advertising world, Tyler barely believed that he would be able to live up to his resolve. But he did, somehow. At fifty-five "he called together his associates and heard himself saying, 'Look, I want out. . . .'" And he retired—to write. Adds Sheehy: "Tyler still carries a tie around in his pocket, but he has stopped wearing it." (Gail Sheehy, *Passages,* p. 504; Bantam Books, Inc., 1977.)

Sometime in the 1950's there was a corporation president who, like Gail Sheehy's Tyler, could hardly wait to retire. His ideal for retirement was not another career but well-earned leisure—in a lovely, properly refurbished, old New England farm house. He did retire, eagerly and in fine

19

health, at the usual age of sixty-five. Within no more than a year, he nearly went insane, literally. I forget the man's name but I did read and greatly enjoy his book, written after this experience, entitled *Chairman of the Bored.*

The first funeral I ever conducted was for a man who, like Horatio Alger, had worked himself up from messenger boy to vice-president of a large international firm. He was only in his early fifties when conflict erupted in the management team. The man was persuaded, no doubt under considerable duress, to take early retirement. He put up a brave front but, within a few years, after a tragic struggle well concealed from all except his wife and children, he was dead. He had committed suicide on the installment plan, by hitting the bottle.

Retirement affects people in a variety of ways.

Ambivalent Forerunner

John the Baptist has long stood forth as the man who was ready to retire. We have come to know and to revere him as the forerunner of Jesus. He was eager to yield the stage, delighted to welcome his successor.

We first meet John as a prophet in his own right, a desert puritan calling people to repentance in the manner of the great prophets of old, Amos or Micah. But, while these earlier prophets proclaimed that the Messiah would come in God's own appointed time, John was preaching that the Messiah's coming was imminent and that he, John, was merely a voice crying in the wilderness, "Prepare the way of the Lord!"

When people began to wonder whether perhaps John himself was the promised Savior, he became angry. "Don't be foolish," he said. "The Messiah, who is coming, is so much greater than I that I am not fit to untie his sandal straps!"

Next, according to the Gospel of the other John, John the Baptist glimpses Jesus at a distance, but that glimpse is sufficient for him. "Behold," John exclaims; "Behold, the Lamb of God, who takes away the sin of the world!" (John 1:29.) Once again, it is evident that John desires nothing more than to "decrease" so that the Lamb of God may "increase."

Then follows the glorious scene of the baptism of Jesus at the hands of John. In that unique moment, when Jesus hears his heavenly Father's voice and feels the Spirit descend on him like a dove, John is certain beyond a doubt that here indeed is the promised Savior. His own happy retirement is imminent.

This is the official version: John the Baptist, forerunner of Jesus the Christ, sent only to herald the Lord's coming, eager to yield his place to the Lord.

But there is another version, a less familiar side of John's relationship with Jesus. It is all there in the Gospels, but we have tended to accept the picture of John as the man ready to retire, without paying attention to other passages. They indicate that John was far from ready to retire. And as for recognizing Jesus as the promised Messiah, John fluctuated wildly between glad assurance and uneasy doubt.

Nor did John withdraw from his ministry after Jesus began his. Rather, within a short time, John's disciples and the disciples of our Lord were in each other's hair. We do not know in what accents John talked about Jesus during this conflict. I like to believe that he tried to temper the ill temper of his followers, because he could not forget his own initial response to Jesus. But I have no proof for my belief. Instead, we have the well-reported episode of John's sending an embassy to Jesus in order to ask him, "Are you he who is to come, or shall we look for another?" (Luke 7:19.)

What further proof of John's ambivalence do we need? If John had been able to hold on to the conviction he felt at the time of our Lord's baptism, that embassy would have had to step forth over his own dead body!

To clinch the matter, we know from later sources, both Christian and pagan, that a sect claiming John as its founder continued for generations after the death and resurrection of our Lord, in stubborn rivalry with the early church. John was long since dead. He had died a martyr's death at the command of Herod Antipas. But while John was thus forcibly "retired," his disciples would not quit, just as he himself had been unwilling to quit, even while claiming that he could hardly wait to yield the stage to his successor.

Decrease, Increase

How do these less familiar facts about John affect our appreciation of him? Paradoxically, they accomplish for us what John so insistently said he wanted, even though he only half meant it. They cause John to decrease in our regard, making him more lifelike, more human, while our admiration for Jesus increases correspondingly. Seen in the light of the whole New Testament, John the Baptist ceases to be a plaster saint and becomes a man: a strange, brave, mixed-up man with whom we can both empathize and sympathize.

John has his own ideas of prophecy and of the prophet's task. He follows the best models: Elijah, Amos,

Jeremiah. He is courageous, blunt, rough. With traditional country bias, he views the wicked big city with jaundiced eyes. He preaches a "come-outer" gospel of deep moral earnestness and profound compassion for the victims of man's inhumanity to man. And he expects Messiah to be like himself, only more so!

When Jesus comes on the scene, John is both awed and puzzled. He knows that the time to step down is near because there is now someone who will carry on, someone with fresh ideas and new approaches. But John also wonders. Does this successor really have what it takes? Can he be expected to show the same commitment to the cause that he, John, has shown? Is this Jesus the right messiah for the job?

In the final analysis, John's painful ambivalence has far more to do with his own destiny than with the fitness or unfitness of his successor. Every retirement is a mini-death. For anyone accustomed to center stage, it is hard enough to step aside, even a few paces. To exit—into the wings—is a form of dying! And the same John who, just a short time later, would be ready to die a martyr's death, did not know how to retire—and live.

Facing this achingly human John, the grandeur of our Lord stands forth all the more boldly. Jesus knew that John's approach would not work. The prophets had all preached in vain. In their lifetime, they were all rejected. They were not able to persuade their people and thus save them from the judgment at hand: from the Assyrians, the Babylonians, the Romans. Jesus knew his people's history. But he also knew, by God-given intuition, that he must follow a different course and that, with him and through him, all things would be different: judgment, redemption, the Kingdom of God, everything.

But Jesus refuses to "put down" John. When that pitiful little embassy from John arrives, Jesus does not say, "You blind fools, stop wasting your time with a man who has had it! You want to be where the action is? Join me!" No, Jesus simply tells them, "Look around. Look at what I am doing—at what my disciples and I are doing. Then judge for yourselves." Not one slurring word about John, not a sign of impatience, no trace of annoyance. On the contrary, every time Jesus makes a comment about John and his work, it is a tribute—a generous, heartfelt tribute to a prophet, a true man of God, an ally in God's Kingdom work.

When at last Jesus receives the news of John's death, he withdraws "in a boat to a lonely place" (Matt. 14:13). Why? Why does he not seize his chance to offer a glowing eulogy and then, at once, straighten out the record? I believe that Jesus, having loved and praised John during his lifetime, felt no need to indulge in eulogies, which could no longer be of help. As for straightening out the record, Jesus preferred to leave that task to God, letting his ministry and—eventually—his crucifixion and resurrection speak for themselves.

To Exit with Grace

Hungary's greatest lyric poet of this century, Endre Ady, has a bitter poem entitled "He Who Shall Take My Place." He begins by asking:

> Is it possible?
> Is it possible that there will be
> another fiery summer,
> nights with falling stars,

> and that I,
> I will no longer be alive?

He goes on with a heartrendingly beautiful pageant of delights, simple delights reserved for the living, which he, being dead, will no longer be able to enjoy. And he concludes with a dreadful curse:

> Let him who takes my place
> be accursed!
> Let poison drip on his tongue!
> Let his eyes be darkened!
> Let his heartbeat stop!
> Blindly let him grope about!
> And if he can find a woman,
> Let him fail to satisfy her!*

Every retirement, from poetry or prophecy, from corporate power or parental authority, is a mini-death. We may say that we are ready, even eager, to be relieved of our responsibilities. We may even believe that we are ready. But are we really? A truly graceful surrender of any status, a genuinely gracious exit from any stage in life, is a hard act. It is also a great challenge, especially for Christians.

It is not easy to be a generous successor, either. We have a great deal to learn from the grace of Jesus toward John, "poor old John," whose place he was taking. But in that role, graciousness is more readily possible.

Things are quite different, however, when we are poor old John; or poor old Boss, about to retire; or poor old Dad, whose children not only do not take his advice anymore but will not even listen to it!

---

*Author's translation from memory.

How shall we perform when the time comes for us to decrease so that another, or others, may increase? We cannot avoid those ambivalent feelings, those vexing changes of mood—and mind. We cannot even hope to negotiate the transition painlessly. It will hurt: every little death of this sort hurts. But it need not destroy us.

Surrender of status, of power, of life itself, can be a step up rather than down—a step up to a higher plane of life. Christian faith furnishes us with a perfect model of this paradox of victory through self-surrender. The same Jesus of Nazareth—who could have been anything he wanted to be, who could have accomplished anything he set his heart on—after a life of just thirty-three years chose a cross.

He could have fought back. He could have mounted a white charger instead of a gray donkey and ridden, no doubt, to the same earthly finale: death on a cross. But had he done so, he would no more be remembered today than would those two other men who were crucified with him. He would have been just one more Zealot, one more Jewish patriot, bitter-ending it in the futile struggle against Rome.

But unlike John, unlike most of us, Jesus knew both when to retire and how to retire. By his divinely graceful exit, he bequeathed to his successors, the apostles, a legacy of divine grace sufficient for them—and for us as well.

3

THE SAMARITAN WOMAN
She Was Looking for a Faith

John 4:1–42

In 1971, Angela Davis was indicted as accessory to a murder. While she was waiting to be tried (and eventually acquitted), an agency of my denomination, the United Presbyterian Church, contributed ten thousand dollars toward her defense. The action caused a deep rift within the church. While personally disapproving of what was done, I could not quarrel with the words of a friend who said: "Angela needs the strongest possible defense. Remember —she has three strikes against her. She is black. She is a woman. And she is a Communist."

From the standpoint of any good Jew, the Samaritan woman in the fourth chapter of John's Gospel also had three strikes against her. She was a Samaritan, a half-Jewish, half-pagan mixed breed despised by the Jews. She was a woman—in a relentlessly patriarchal society. And she was a pariah, not because of her politics but because there had been, to put it kindly, too many men in her life.

But this woman with three strikes against her was also, perhaps unknown to herself, a seeker, in search of a faith. What kind of faith was she seeking? From her conversation with Jesus at Jacob's well, near the Samaritan village of Sychar where she lived, the contours of the faith she hoped to find appear clearly and poignantly.

Antidote to Self-Rejection

The woman was looking, first of all, for a faith that would help her overcome her self-rejection. Samaritans were second-class people in the eyes of all Jews. This, however, caused them to feel like third-class people because the Jews themselves were second-class people at the time, mere vassals of their Roman overlords.

The Samaritans had no slogan like "Samaritan Is Beautiful!" They did not feel that way about themselves. Just as most American blacks, before the advent of "Black Is Beautiful," had accepted the white stereotype of them and responded to it with self-doubt and self-loathing, so had the Samaritans vis-à-vis the Jews. Being told they were inferior and being treated as inferiors for hundreds of years, most Samaritans had come to reject themselves as inferior.

But we need not be members of a national or ethnic minority to be acquainted with self-rejection. For the last decade or so we have come increasingly to experience a pervasive feeling of powerlessness—the powerlessness of individuals in a mass society run by faceless forces. Frustrations pile up, but there seems to be no one on whom to vent them. The feeling was highlighted dramatically in the motion picture *Network*. In it a concerned television commentator (who eventually goes insane) urges his audience to lean out of their windows at an agreed-upon hour and yell into the streets, "I am mad as hell and I am not going to take it anymore!" Millions respond—with predictable, pathetic futility! Wondering whether anyone pays attention to us, whether we even matter as individual human beings, can sap our ego strength as much as suffering group discrimination. The more we tell ourselves that there is little or nothing we can do—even by getting "mad as hell"—and that we really do not count as persons, the more we become mired in self-rejection.

What did Jesus offer the Samaritan woman as an antidote for her self-rejection? He offered her a fresh sense of her worth as a person. She knew that Jesus had no business even talking with her. Was he not a Jew and she a Samaritan? Was he not a man, a learned man, and she a woman—and no paragon of womanhood at that? But Jesus did not "put her down." He responded to her simply, graciously, personally. He gave her a sense of herself as a child of God, a unique and worthwhile human being. Suddenly she felt free to talk, because someone important considered it worth his while to listen to her.

The woman was also looking for a faith that would help her overcome her skepticism. Most skeptics are rather wistful people. They are skeptical not because they think it is smart to be so, but because they have been disillusioned—by people, by false gods, by people peddling false gods. The Samaritan woman was a wistful skeptic. When she asked Jesus where he proposed to get that "living water" (that is, spring water instead of rain water stagnating at the bottom of a cistern), she was not being sarcastic. She had simply come to doubt all promises, because she had believed in too many that were broken, including some that had broken her heart. She did not want to be lifted up once more only to be let down with a sickening thud.

What Jesus had to offer the Samaritan woman at this point was not "proof." He had no proof, in that sense.

Christian faith has no proof, either. Christian faith is just that— faith. Any faith worthy of the name includes—by definition—a generous margin for doubt. Faith in Jesus Christ is not based on a series of irrefutable propositions. It is based on a gamble of trust in a Person. What Jesus was asking the Samaritan woman—and all the others he was calling to become disciples—was in effect to bet her life on him. Or, rather, it was to bet her life on God because of *his* faith in God. As an antidote for the woman's skepticism, Jesus offered her a challenge based on his own faith.

If you feel that you cannot pray because you are not sure you believe in God, you may consider praying just because Jesus prayed and he was no fool. Or you might try praying, anyway, on the advice of the great nineteenth-century preacher, Horace Bushnell: "Pray to the dim God, confessing the dimness for honesty's sake." Or you might use the words of a nameless, equally wistful fellow skeptic: "O God, if you exist, help me, if you can!" But when you suddenly perceive God in the face of Jesus, your fumbling attempts at prayer get on target. They become sharp, focused. This is what happened to Saul—a devout Jew but, at bottom, a profoundly wistful skeptic —when God put on flesh for him, in Jesus of Nazareth. Thereafter it was no longer "I know *what* I have believed" but "I know *whom* I have believed." But by that time Saul had become Paul.

Again, the Samaritan woman was looking for a faith that would help her overcome her fatigue. Whatever Jesus might mean by "living water," whether he would tap a special spring just for her or perform some other miracle, the woman could see one practical advantage in the gracious offer: it would make her life easier. Jacob's well, which is still in use, is one of the deepest wells in the land.

In ancient times it may have been one hundred feet deep. That daily walk, with her long rope, bucket, and large earthenware jug, was getting to be too much for her, especially since she chose to come at high noon. She was getting on in years, and was bone tired, not just physically but spiritually. The drabness of her life had gotten her down as much as its physical strain. She could do with some indoor plumbing!

We sympathize—even though we do have indoor plumbing, and hundreds of other labor-saving devices—because we have substituted new frustrations for old ones. Our gadgets do not work much of the time, and even when they do work they need to be tended, "serviced," which is just as boring as doing the work the hard way—and far less invigorating. In addition, we have invented thousands of new, boring jobs—like filing pieces of paper, and like punching cards or tape. And when our working time is cut back, or when at last we retire, we manage to be bored with our free time!

The antidote Jesus has to offer for physical and spiritual fatigue is not a magic formula to put a thrill into every chore but a perspective to make the unavoidable endurable. We may never attain the powers of concentration Brother Lawrence developed when he taught himself to peel potatoes to the glory of God in that monastery kitchen. But the only effective counterattack on weariness and boredom and the weariness of boredom will be a mental one. If my mind is filled with the love of God that I have experienced in Jesus Christ, I will be able to think about people, pray for people, and minister to people, while doing justice to the chores at hand.

The Samaritan woman was also looking for a faith that would help her overcome her moral confusion. Just as she was about to start a solid, and safely abstract, theological discussion with Jesus (about the proper place for worship, whether on Mount Zion or Mount Gerizim), Jesus cut her short with the apparent *non sequitur:* "Bring your husband here!" It has been conjectured that Jesus said this because he remembered that a rabbi was not supposed to talk with a woman alone, anywhere, for any length of time lest there be gossip. But Jesus paid little heed to such matters when a person's needs were at stake. If he had, he would not have taken the route that led through Samaria in the first place. He would have gladly trudged the few extra miles, as did most good Jews, to avoid contact with the Samaritans.

No, by asking the woman to fetch her husband, Jesus put his finger on her self-esteem's most painful sore. Why did this woman come to the well at midday, when the sun was boring holes through even the best-veiled skull? Because her "private life" had made her an outcast. She had had five "husbands" and was now living with an equally dubious sixth; and she did not respect herself for her performance!

The antidote Jesus offers us when we have begun to become aware of our moral confusion is an exposure, guaranteed to hurt, of our excuses, our subterfuges, our rationalizations. Remember how Simon Peter reacted when he discovered who Jesus really was? He exclaimed: "Depart from me, for I am a sinful man, O Lord." (Luke 5:8.) He could not have blurted out anything more to the point. So often, when I say "I cannot believe in God," I really mean "I cannot stop cheating on my wife" or "I cannot give up my job even though I know it is crooked, rotten to the core: it pays too well"! Just as often theological quibbling is merely a smoke screen for moral confusion, guilt, and shame. These, when exposed, call for repentance—and forgiveness.

Finally, the Samaritan woman was looking for a faith that would help her transcend her present inadequate religion. Jesus Christ never comes into a vacuum. He always encounters and displaces some previously held faith. There were few atheists, if any, in Palestine in our Lord's day. By and large, the Hebrew Law was honored, and there was considerable expectancy of the promised Messiah. But many devout Jews were restless in their ancient faith—hence the response to Jesus of the few who dared openly to follow him, and of the many more who, like Nicodemus, wished they dared. The Samaritan woman, however, possessed only a mongrelized version of the Jewish faith. For her, the Law was largely a burden, seldom if ever a source of joy. For her, the promised Messiah was no more than a ticket on the Irish sweepstakes, symbol of a remote hope of unearned good times, Santa Claus on a white horse. The woman's quest for a vital faith, half-unconscious as it was, was handicapped rather than assisted by her Samaritan-Jewish religion.

During more than twenty years, as pastor of various churches, I would lead inquirers groups for persons who claimed to be ready to examine the Christian faith in order to find out whether perchance it was the right faith for them. I met few atheists in the groups, and positively no visitors from outer space. In other words, I was working with "lapsed" Christians, nominal Christians, Christians who knew as much (or as little) about Christianity as did the members of those churches, but who had given up Christian practice. They had stopped praying, stopped reading the Bible, stopped attending worship. At some point in their lives, remembered or forgotten, they had been "turned off." Now they were willing at least to take a second look.

What we did in those inquirers groups was no mystery, nor did it work like magic. We did some reading and we discussed what we read—self-consciously at first, then with growing trust and openness. Before long, people would begin to talk about their present "religions"—and their dissatisfaction with them. Just as the Samaritan woman's religion was a mongrelized Judaism, most people in these groups—whether by themselves or through participation in offshoots of historic Christianity (e.g., Mormonism, Christian Science)—had arrived at some substitute gospel that was not the Gospel.

The antidote Jesus offered to the Samaritan woman for her inadequate religion was not a "putdown." He took her where she was and respectfully discussed her religious beliefs with her. Working with them, he helped her discover their inadequacy—in terms of her own unavowed, perhaps largely unrealized, dissatisfaction. Finally she was ready to respond to him, and to *his* faith in God, not just intellectually but personally.

This is what we were striving for, and sometimes, by God's grace, were able to trigger in those inquirers groups: a truly personal rather than a merely intellectual response to God's claim through Jesus Christ. This personal response was to be the Samaritan woman's final reaction to her encounter with Jesus. What had turned her around was not his theological acumen, nor even his graciousness, but that he had revealed her whole life to her in a new light. "He told me all that I ever did" (John 4:39), the woman told her amazed, skeptical fellow villagers. She might have added: "And what I could do, even now, at this late date, to make my life count for something!" But she did not need to elaborate. Her few friends—and many despisers—*saw* the difference in her!

The Samaritan woman had three strikes against her. She was a Samaritan. She was a woman. And she was a moral mess. In addition, she was a dully average person: provincial, working class, poor. But somewhere beneath that unpromising exterior there was a seeker. God had struck a spark of creative restlessness in her soul that Jesus fanned into a living flame because he cared and was willing to take the time. To use the lovely metaphor of the story itself, Jesus provided for the thirst of her soul that unique "living water"—himself—which would satisfy her for the rest of her life, and for eternity.

4

THE PHARISEE
At Least He Tried

Luke 18:9–14

"Two men went up into the temple to pray. . . ." A glorious story—and a deeply biased story. Jesus meant it that way. He placed the full weight of judgment on the Pharisee's shoulders, while he covered the shoulders of the publican with the mantle of God's grace.

When Jesus invited his hearers to eavesdrop on the prayers of these two men, he clearly intended to portray the Pharisee as a man who prayed wrong. Jesus wanted to make one point and only one: that pride goes before a fall, while penitence gives God a chance. So we have been cheering for the publican and despising the Pharisee ever since.

The story assumes that the publican was sincere and that the Pharisee was a hypocrite. But a story is a story. So we may have the right, for once, to assume the exact opposite! Let us assume, then, that the Pharisee was sincere and the publican a hypocrite. After all, Jesus did not deal in stereotypes—ever. He did not intend the story as a wholesale whitewashing of publicans. The record shows

Reprinted from *Presbyterian Life,* November 15, 1963. Used by permission of A.D. Publications Incorporated.

that Jesus, in spite of his severe criticism of Pharisaism, welcomed and enjoyed the friendship of many Pharisees.

Negative Virtue

The first thing that strikes us about this Pharisee's prayer is the negative tenor of its opening. "God, I thank thee that I am *not* like other men." Of course, we are offended. We have been conditioned to seeing the worst in this man. But now we are assuming that he is not being hypocritical—that he is being sincere. In this perspective, his thankfulness to God because he has not committed certain sins, while still a little arrogant, takes on a brighter hue.

The Pharisee prays: "God, I thank thee that I am not like other men, . . . extortioners." The Law of Moses was full of rules governing the conduct of business. Wherever there are rules, there are ways to get around them. If a Jewish businessman happened to be both devout and conscientious, he was in for a hard time. If he was devout, a true student of the Law, he knew all the rules—and all the loopholes. If he was conscientious, his conscience bade him ignore the loopholes and stay within the intent of the rules to the detriment of his competitive position. For this day-by-day contest between his hunger for profit and his thirst for divine approval he needed strength, spiritual strength. Is it so wrong, then, that our Pharisee, insofar as he had been able to master many temptations, should wish to give thanks to God—for that strength?

The Pharisee prays: "God, I thank thee that I am not like other men, . . . adulterers." The Law of Moses, once again, abounded in rules for the sexual life—rules too numerous and too detailed to suit us. We are being told

today, from all sides, that there are no rules to govern
sexual conduct, that there ought to be no rules for whatever "consenting adults" enjoy doing with each other,
that a person's sex life is no one's business except his or
her own. By this standard or, rather, lack of standard, the
Pharisees were surely an "uptight" lot. They were trying
to search out and to obey God's standard for sexual behavior, embodied in the Law, according to which there
were only two morally, socially, and spiritually acceptable
options: continence or monogamous marriage.

Over against this demanding standard, however, the
Pharisees were also flesh-and-blood men living among all
the normal temptations common to all ages. Nor did the
majority of less scrupulous Jews and unscrupulous
Samaritans make it any easier for the Pharisees to adhere
to Mosaic virtue. Insofar, then, as our Pharisee had been
able with God's help to resist sexual temptation, it would
hardly be fair to criticize him for thanking God, the source
of his resistance.

Once again, the Pharisee prays: "I thank thee, God,
that I am not . . . unjust." This is clearly the most offensive
of the three negative thanksgivings. Here is a man who
seems to be saying: "I have kept the whole Law!" Knowing something about the Law of Moses, about its intricacy
and severity, we exclaim: "How could he? How could
anyone? How does he have the nerve to make such a
preposterous claim?"

True, no one could possibly keep the whole Law of
Moses, let alone the whole Law of God. In this light, the
Pharisee's self-assurance is indeed repugnant. However,
we can say, we *must* say this for him: *at least he tried!* He
tried so hard that he seemed to have convinced himself of
his own success. Is it so irredeemably bad, then, that inso-

far as he believed he had been successful, he should give God the credit and the praise?

Beyond the Line of Duty

The Pharisees loved the Law. Read Psalm 119 to catch the flavor of that love. They considered themselves the successors of Ezra and of the early scribes who drafted the Law as an emblem of Jewish identity and a bulwark of Jewish survival. Had it not been for these "Separatists" (for that is what the word "Pharisees" means), Judaism might have vanished after the Exile—and again after the destruction of Jerusalem by the Romans, in A.D. 70.

The Law, which the Pharisees loved, was tough. The reward for keeping the Law was a sense of "rightness" with God—with its inevitable temptation to self-right-eousness, to which the Pharisees so widely succumbed (see Matthew 23). But the Pharisees did not expect others to do anything they would not do themselves. On the contrary, many of them insisted, voluntarily, on doing more than the Law required. They were all trying to please God by perfectly obeying the Law, but some of them tried for beyond-the-line-of-duty obedience.

The Pharisee in our story seems to have been one of those. He thanked God in view of all the temptations to which he had not succumbed. Then, at once, he went on to remind God of all the extra "good works" he was doing.

He was fasting twice a week. The rank and file of the Jews were required to fast only on the high holy days. Only the most devout fasted twice a week, Mondays and Thursdays. Did they enjoy fasting? Hardly. But that does not mean that our Pharisee fasted twice a week only for the sake of earthly prestige and heavenly reward. Having

resolved to credit him with sincerity, there is no reason for
us to doubt that, like Jesus himself, the Pharisee found in
fasting a valuable spiritual discipline. Those of us who
have tried from time to time to fast as an expression of our
concern with world hunger have probably discovered unsuspected spiritual values in the practice. And, for all we
know, the Pharisee may have given the money he was
saving on food on Mondays and Thursdays to the poor!

He also excelled in tithing. He was giving to the Temple a full tenth not only of his grain and fruit, which was
required, but of all his income, which was not required.
Once again, we wonder about the Pharisee's motives.
Would we not be highly suspicious of a man who voluntarily overpaid his taxes, whether to the IRS or to the
Almighty? Of course we would!

But is it not true that a citizen who pays his taxes to
the last shekel or beyond is likely to care more deeply
about his country than his neighbor who is using every
means, both legal and shady, to trim his tax burden?

And is it not true that a Christian who gives to the
church more than appears necessary by any conventional
reckoning is likely to care more deeply about the church
than his fellow Christian who contributes that meanest of
fictions, "the average"?

It is difficult to believe that the Pharisee would have
voluntarily exceeded his tithe solely because of the ego
inflation it brought him. If his motives were mixed (and
whose motives are not?), some of them had to be good. For
instance, he would feel that he was setting a worthy example for his fellow Jews. Or he might feel a more "pro-
prietary" love for the Temple and its glorious worship.
Either way, his giving beyond the required tithe would be
an expression of his love for God.

But if the Pharisee's thanksgiving for his extra "good works" sounds, to say the least, immodest, his attitude toward the publican seems unforgivably offensive. It is indeed pharisaical in the worst sense of a notoriously bad word. "God, I thank thee," he prays, "that I am not like . . . this publican"! Surely this is enough to hang him, no matter how much sincerity we may attribute to him—and to credit him with sincerity is, after all, the faintest of faint praises. How can we possibly forgive the Pharisee's blatant, self-righteous contempt for the publican?

Right—but not so fast. Publicans were men who had bought concessions from the Roman government for the collection of taxes, in exchange for a percentage of all taxes collected. They were doing the dirtiest dirty work for the oppressors of their people, for a fat profit. No wonder all decent Jews hated and despised them.

We might wish that the Pharisee had prayed, "God, make me an instrument of redemption for this publican." But since this was beyond him, we cannot altogether condemn him for praying, with genuine gratitude in his heart, "God, I thank thee that I am not like this publican."

Cheap Grace

But the publican *repented!* There he stands, eyes downcast, knees shaking, hands thumping on chest in the traditional gesture of penitence. He is praying a prayer of confession, which was touchingly different from the Pharisee's prayer of thanksgiving. Clearly, the publican was praying *right;* and is not that what matters?

Remember: we are assuming that the Pharisee was sincere and the publican hypocritical. And why not? Who is to say that the latter really meant business about his repentance?

Zacchaeus did. He was a publican. But when Jesus called him, he responded by *doing* something. What he said, whether he offered even a word of prayer, is not recorded. Zacchaeus acted on his repentance, at once. He began making the rounds of his "accounts," his victims, going from door to door the length and breadth of Jericho like a reverse Every Home Canvass, not collecting money but refunding his "percentage" with interest!

Did the people applaud his repentance? I doubt it. I rather think that they accepted the refund and despised the man, not just for having been a crook but perhaps even more for turning out to be a "softie"! But Zacchaeus did not expect to receive divine forgiveness without consequence or obligation. Rather, having received it free— as God's free gift, which it always is—he set out at once to "pay" for it, freely and joyfully.

But Zacchaeus was not typical. The typical publican was more like today's typical Protestant: long on prayer, short on action. We have learned the lesson of the Reformation well; so well, in fact, that we have unlearned it! We recite over and over that we are saved not by "good works" but *sola fide,* by faith alone. We look with puzzlement at our orthodox Jewish neighbors who continue to live "under the Law," with all its inconveniences including a kosher diet. We are self-righteously disturbed by the legalism of conservative Roman Catholics and the militant strictness of the Mormons. We are deeply uneasy about fellow Protestants who inflict upon themselves—poor, benighted souls—such rigors as a literal tithe, abstention from drinking and smoking—and regular, vocal witness to their faith!

But what are *we* doing? In the name of justification by faith, that great Reformation text, we have just about given up "good works"! Few of us practice any specifically Christian discipline, partly because we look down on the "naïve" disciplines of fellow Christians, largely because we are too self-indulgent to devise and adopt suitably "mature" disciplines for ourselves. The assurance of God's free grace has become, in our hands, an alibi for do-little or do-nothing discipleship.

The Pharisee was trying, trying hard, to obey God's Law, to do God's will according to his own, admittedly limited, and perhaps self-serving, understanding. The publican, however, went through the motions of a prayer of confession, just as we do, usually in hurried unison, every Sunday morning. The next day, he returned to his office, relieved—and unchanged. This is what Dietrich Bonhoeffer, the German pastor, theologian, and martyr, called "cheap grace." "Cheap grace," wrote Bonhoeffer in *The Cost of Discipleship,* "is the preaching of forgiveness without requiring repentance; baptism without Church discipline; Communion without confession; absolution without contrition. Cheap grace is grace without discipleship, grace without the Cross, grace without Jesus Christ, living and incarnate." (Dietrich Bonhoeffer, "Costly Grace," *The Cost of Discipleship,* p. 38; The Macmillan Company, 1948.)

Is this dangerous doctrine? Are we likely to forfeit justification by faith and relapse into justification by works? Is Bonhoeffer tempting us to forsake the publican's blush for the Pharisee's flush? To me, the danger seems remote. For the moment, we have more to learn from the Pharisee than from the publican.

True, Saul of Tarsus discovered the freedom of God's

grace—but only after he had literally exhausted his strength in observing the Jewish Law. True, Augustine of Hippo rediscovered the freedom of God's grace—but only after he had spent decades earnestly trying to fulfill the exacting demands of several systems of philosophy. True, Martin Luther made his "protest" in the name of the freedom of God's grace—but only after he had spent all his young manhood in the strictest monastic discipline.

The parable of the Pharisee and the publican is basic gospel. Luke—and Paul—are faithful to the central message of Jesus when they stress human sinfulness and free, unmerited grace. But the good news of God's free grace must be brought into bifocal perspective with the message of The Epistle of James: "Faith without works is dead"!

If I were asked to compose epitaphs for the Pharisee and the publican, I would write for the Pharisee "AT LEAST HE TRIED," and for the tax collector "DID HE EVEN TRY?"

In this bifocal perspective, what will be your epitaph?

5

ZACCHAEUS

The Man
Who Had Everything

Luke 19:1–10

On a fine autumn day I was treating a friend from New
York to a sight-seeing cruise around Marin County, San
Francisco's delightful suburb. It was a golden afternoon.
The leaves had just begun to turn. Driving at a painfully
law-abiding speed on a tree-shaded avenue, we saw a
gentleman gallantly easing his lady into a Lincoln Conti-
nental. The lady was lovely, the Lincoln even lovelier. The
setting sun cast an approving glow over the scene. My
friend, overcome with a mixture of emotions, groaned:
"That man! He's got everything! He's got a Lincoln. He's
got a beautiful woman. And he lives in Marin County!"

Many such groans could be heard just out of earshot,
or perhaps within earshot, of Zacchaeus, little Mr. Big of
lovely Jericho. He also was the man who had everything.
Zacchaeus did not have to worry about how much he
would have left after taxes. His chief worry was that the
citizens of Jericho should have enough left after taxes—
for next year's taxes. Zacchaeus had everything money
could buy—and why should "everything" not include a

First published in 1972 by Cathedral Publishers, Royal Oak, Michigan.
Reprinted by permission.

beautiful woman? Or several? Zacchaeus lived in Jericho, the "city of palms." There stood the sumptuous palace of Herod the Great overlooking palatial villas with park-like gardens. Jericho, the "pantry of Jerusalem," was the quintessential suburb. Indeed, Zacchaeus had everything. Or did he?

Dead End for Zacchaeus

One thing Zacchaeus did not have and could not buy: he could not add another foot to his stature. To be a little too short or a little too tall may seem a minor handicap for practical purposes, but it can have major psychological effects. It is likely that Zacchaeus worked harder because he was unable to accept himself, all five feet of his tubby self. He regarded himself as ungainly, unjustly treated by the celestial Department of Weights and Measures, and at an unfair disadvantage with his fellowmen. As a result, he did what many of us with real or imagined handicaps are apt to do: he overcompensated. He felt compelled to prove to the world that he was as much of a man as any perfect physical specimen. His self-rejection had turned him into a human dynamo, driving himself and others with utter ruthlessness.

This drive for recognition had made him plunge into the money game, because he could not imagine that anyone would ever like him, let alone love him, just for himself. He cultivated cynicism as carefully as one would cultivate a rare, tender plant. It did not take him long to discover that money can buy just about everything, including a reasonable facsimile of the things it supposedly cannot buy.

To be sure, Zacchaeus knew that very few people

approved of him. But he had taught himself not to care as long as they served his interest or pleasure. He also knew, in rare moments of honesty, that he could count his friends on one hand, with all the fingers chopped off. But, through all the years of struggle, jockeying, and climbing, he kept his misgivings mostly well hidden from himself.

The time came, however, when his motor began to show signs of wear. As so often happens, he had arrived at the top with all four tires of his ego beautifully inflated, hardly aware of their dangerously threadbare condition. Along the road, he had been so busy cutting corners that he never heard as much as a single piston knock from his conscience. What is more, his climb along the winding road to business eminence had been so rapid that the stench of the exhaust could not rise fast enough to catch his nostrils and warn him of the moral pollutants that were eating away his soul.

Now he was at the top. He had arrived. He possessed all the things of which he was afraid life would cheat him. He had made a place for himself under the sun, a regular private solarium. He was not the mayor of Jericho, but he could pull all the strings which make mayors jump. He was disliked but accepted; envied but secure. He lived in the finest neighborhood, belonged to all the right clubs, and even his ulcer did not bother him overmuch.

Then, without warning, Zacchaeus was fifty. Or fifty-five. Or whatever the critical age may have been in his day among men of his stamp. Having time to relax, he realized that this was a skill he had never learned. Having a chance to reflect, he was dismayed by his unsuspected reflections. Somewhat flatteringly but with growing uneasiness, Zacchaeus began comparing himself with that unknown philosopher of his people known simply as "Ecclesiastes" or "the Preacher," who had written: "Vanity of vanities! All is vanity"!

A Visit from Jesus

What moved Zacchaeus to make rather a fool of himself by climbing a tree in an attempt to see Jesus? Perhaps he thought it was idle curiosity. Perhaps he was taking a long chance on satisfying some hidden hunger, some vitamin deficiency of the spirit, that his rich fare of high living had left within him. Or perhaps he had sunk to such a depth of boredom that he was ready to welcome anything —spiritualism, Soka Gakkai, LSD—anything that promised speedy and painless relief.

We shall never know what took place between Jesus and Zacchaeus during those few moments that changed Zacchaeus' life. There is no need to speculate on how Jesus knew, nor on the hidden resources that enabled Zacchaeus to respond to him. What we have on record is complete in itself.

What Jesus did was to release Zacchaeus from the judgments in which he was trapped. Through the years Zacchaeus had successfully pretended that he did not care about what people thought of him. Yet during all that time he had never been able to escape the slow, deep-drilling pain of their contempt for him. No one is immune to the judgment of his fellowmen. If we say that we do not care about being respected and loved, we only show that we neither love nor respect ourselves, that we are self-condemned. Judged by friend and foe alike as a crook and a hypocrite, Zacchaeus was trapped in a cage of self-loathing wired with the alternating current of self-infatuation and self-hate.

But Jesus said: "Zacchaeus, come down! I want to stay with you today." With one stroke, Jesus released Zacchaeus from the contempt of his fellows as well as from his own self-condemnation. For the first time in his life, Zacchaeus was receiving an offer of spontaneous, disinterested, unsought friendship. That alone might have changed the course of his life. The fact that the offer came from Jesus did the rest.

For Jesus' offer of friendship is never a cozy, comfortable proposition. It will not fit neatly into our personal and social *status quo.* A man once asked me about what he should do, beyond continuing in his responsible position in a major industry, in order to give himself the assurance of more significant accomplishment. He said, in substance: "I've been giving about five percent of my time to the Lord. Now I can afford about fifteen percent. How do I go about it?"

This is not how it works! You cannot give the Lord of life a carefully calculated percentage of what you feel you can spare of your time or money or energy. You cannot enlist with the Lord on your own terms. He drafts you—on his terms. I believe that my five-percent man is still calling to Jesus, "Lord, look here, I now have another ten percent of myself to give you!" But the Lord has moved on, looking up strange, unlikely trees for strange, unlikely men—men who are stuck, not on themselves but with themselves—men who, like Zacchaeus, know that only God's grace can unstick them!

Out of the Dead End

Zacchaeus was a contemptible, unhappy person. But when he came face to face with Jesus, he knew that there had to be a complete settlement. No bargaining was possible, no installment plan. He was going to pay up, in full, at once.

The first step would be, in a sense, the easiest. "Lord," Zacchaeus said, "the half of my goods I give to the poor." If he had offered to do nothing more, Jesus might have doubted the man's sincerity. Zacchaeus still had the other half of his fortune—more than enough to live on. A gift of half might have been little more than a pious bribe, an attempt to buy off, in one *beau geste,* the citizens of Jericho, the Master from Nazareth, and his own conscience.

But Zacchaeus went on at once: "and if I have defrauded any one of anything, I restore it fourfold." How much was going to remain of all his wealth after fulfilling this promise? About ten cents, I would guess. But that is still not the most important point. The most important point is that Zacchaeus realized he had to go to his so-called friends, his victims, customers, or whatever they were, *one by one,* receiving little applause and heaps of abuse. But he went through the whole ordeal nonstop; and not with his old business smirk of phony good cheer but with the radiance of a man who had seen the living God in the face of Jesus!

Zacchaeus had been lost—in middle-age boredom, impotent remorse, and engulfing futility, but Jesus had found him and saved him. Zacchaeus had come to believe, with Ecclesiastes, that life was a long series of vain, meaningless acts, and that there was nothing new under the sun. But Jesus broke through the crust of his cynicism and showed Zacchaeus that life, life with him, can truly begin at forty, or at fifty-five, or at any time.

Zacchaeus lived at a time when suicide was not only common but fashionable among the most refined Greeks and Romans. To shorten life either by reckless, intemperate living or by a brave, blasphemous search for death, was considered the proper and civilized thing to do. Into such a world came Jesus, announcing to all who would listen, "I came that they may have life." He brought with him such a zest for life—for his unique kind of self-giving life—that, for the first time in human history, eternity became an object of hope rather than of dread. Anyone who, like Zacchaeus, tasted this new life knew at once that only eternity could do justice to all its possibilities for adventure.

Zacchaeus thought that he had everything, when he had only attained the small, static objectives of his small, static self. In his encounter with Jesus, Zacchaeus saw for the first time the meanness of his attainment and the glorious, ever-expanding horizons toward which the Master would lead him. The eyes of Jesus served Zacchaeus as a kind of mirror in which to see himself in an extraordinary double image, Zacchaeus B.C. and Zacchaeus A.D.—and, Lord, what a change!

6

JUDAS

Jesus' One Wrong Choice?

Matthew 26:14–25; 27:1–5

In Dante's *Inferno,* the lowest pit of hell is not the hottest
place but the coldest. It is a frozen lake composed of
human tears. In this lake lives Satan, a hideous monster
with three heads. In each mouth, Satan is crushing a traitor: Brutus and Cassius on the right and on the left and,
in the central mouth, Judas Iscariot. No other literary or
artistic image expresses more strikingly the horror in
which Judas has been held through the ages. No parents
would name a son Judas. No one would inflict the name
even on a stray dog.

But this Judas, this embodiment of treachery, was
also a man—flesh of our flesh, bone of our bone. What is
more remarkable, he was one of the men whom Jesus had
called to special privilege. Three times in the passion narrative, Matthew refers to Judas as "one of the twelve," as
if he could hardly believe it himself. Whatever Judas became, a mere three years earlier he had been a person of
sufficient promise both to receive and to accept the call of
Jesus Christ.

Reprinted from *Presbyterian Life,* March 1, 1965. Used by permission of
A.D. Publications Incorporated.

The Man Judas

What do we know about this man Judas? The Evangelists do not tell us very much apart from his performance as a traitor. They can hardly be blamed for their silence. They could not and would not look beyond the vileness of his treason. Wherever Judas is mentioned, it is in the context of disapproval and contempt. In fact, he is never mentioned at all without some reference to his treason, as "Judas Iscariot . . . (he who was to betray him)," or "Judas, who betrayed him." It is nearly impossible to catch a reliable view of a person through such a dark screen of hate.

If you were to track down all the clues in all four Gospels regarding the background and character of Judas, you would be even more perplexed because of the man's extraordinary ordinariness. He was a Judean surrounded by eleven Galileans. As a one-man minority, he might well be carrying a chip on his shoulder. It seems, too, that he was rather bright and therefore jealous of the others, especially of Peter, James, and John, who occupied favored places within the circle of the disciples.

There appears to be a dependable consensus that Judas was good with money, or loved money, or most likely both. Still, thirty silver coins in the currency of the day would be too paltry a sum to motivate him, or anyone, to commit such a gross act of treason just for the money.

If money was not the motive, what was? Scholars have been trying to unravel the motivation of Judas, the traitor, but have not come up with anything conclusive. The most widely accepted hypothesis seems to be that Judas was a Zealot, a member of that small, violent sect

of superpatriots who wanted to free their people from the
yoke of Rome by revolution. Judas had his heart set on
Jesus' leading that revolution. He wanted Jesus to become
"King of the Jews." When at last he understood that Jesus
did not seek that kind of kingdom, and that violence was
abhorrent to him, Judas betrayed him. Whether out of
pain and spite, or in order to force Jesus to embrace the
revolution after all—if only to save his own life, since the
Roman authorities had him marked for death on suspicion
of subversive activity—Judas acted. We can only conjecture why. We simply do not know what moved Judas to
do what he did.

Jesus and Judas

Judas was an ordinary traitor, then, committing an act
of treason with obscure motives. Only the victim was
unique! In fact, we do not begin to see either the traitor
or the act of treason clearly until we look at them through
the eyes of the betrayed.

How did Jesus feel about Judas? According to one
version, advocated by the author of the Fourth Gospel,
Jesus picked Judas in the first place because the plot called
for a villain. It is true that the manner in which the plot
unfolds in the Gospels, especially in the Fourth Gospel,
makes Jesus' betrayal by Judas an essential part of the plot.
But to credit Jesus with such advance knowledge of the
whole plot undermines his real humanity—without which
both the cross and the empty tomb lose their meaning.
When the evangelist John suggests that Jesus chose Judas
because someone had to play the traitor's part, he means to
exalt Jesus. But he misses the mark, because anything that
makes Jesus less than fully human debases him.

No, Jesus picked Judas because Judas showed promise as well as zeal. So did the other eleven, in varying degrees. Then, when the pressure rose, one man out of twelve was bound to break—if only by the law of human averages. In a sense, they all betrayed the Master. Peter, the only one who drew the sword in his defense, soon denied ever having known Jesus. Ten others faded into the night. Eventually, John alone was present when Jesus was being tried in the high priest's court. Until the very end, then, Judas had indeed been "one of the twelve," no less human than the rest of them. And Jesus probably loved Judas, as offensive as this might sound, just as he loved the others —in the intimacies of their spiritual apprenticeship, in the excitement of the early apostolic ventures, and in the tension of the steady march of events.

Then, at the Last Supper, Jesus knew. How he had discovered the dreadful truth about Judas we do not know, but it could not have been very difficult. Probably it was written all over Judas' face, except for the specific details of time and place. So, as much to console the eleven as to give the traitor a twinge of sorrow, Jesus said: "The Son of man goes as it is written of him, but woe to that man by whom the Son of man is betrayed! It would have been better for that man if he had not yet been born." (Matt. 26:24.)

There is something movingly deliberate and willing about the Master's surrender to his destiny. Neither Judas nor anyone else can take from him that which he will freely give. The Son of Man sees the shadow of death and advances unafraid; but woe to him who will soon wish that he had never been born, who will soon do his gruesome best to make believe he never was born!

There is no trace of bitterness in Jesus—only the bitter taste of the cup which, for the sake of his mission, he must drain to the dregs. When Judas approaches with the armed mob and kisses the Master in the ghostly light of the torches, Jesus asks: "Friend, why are you here?" (Matt. 26:50.) "Friend!" Jesus is turning the knife in the wound, but his blade is clean. Even the pain he inflicts has a cleansing, surgical effect on the festering conscience of Judas. That word "friend"—and the smile that accompanies it—propel Judas into a frenzy of remorse and out into the dark night of death, so that the most damned death occurs at the same time as the most saving death!

A Clue

But there is still a word to be spoken, a word from the cross. Did Jesus include Judas in his last prayer, "Father, forgive them; for they know not what they do"? In a sense, Judas did not deserve to be included since, of all people, he *knew* what he had done. But does anyone *deserve* to be included in that prayer? Does anyone *deserve* to be forgiven by the Crucified?

We do not know, we cannot know, whether Jesus meant to include Judas, specifically, in his forgiveness. But there is one clue, in the Gospel of John of all places, to suggest that Jesus did mean to forgive Judas, and especially Judas. In what is called his high priestly prayer, Jesus prays, speaking of his disciples: "I have guarded them, and none of them is lost but the son of perdition." (John 17:12.) Thus the usual translation. But the basic meaning of the Greek word rendered "perdition" is not "damnation," but "destruction" or "waste." Perhaps Jesus remembered how Judas had used this very word while ranting about the waste of the perfume that a woman (perhaps Mary Magdalene) had poured over the Master— in beautiful, foolish devotion. Could it be that the disciple most worried about waste had himself become the one waste product of the Master's love? "Son of perdition" does not sound like Jesus. "Son of waste" does. Indeed, Martin Luther follows the purest evangelical instinct when he translates the phrase as "lost child." And what would be more like Jesus than a prayer for Judas using this phrase: "Father, forgive thy lost child"?

Perhaps I have carried this plea for the ordinariness, the humanity, the forgivability of Judas too far. You may not be able to identify at all with Judas and therefore may resent my apparent defense of him. But remember: if you cannot identify with Judas, you must be a better person than any one of the disciples!

How so?

Because, at the Last Supper, when Jesus quietly announced, "One of you is going to betray me," the disciples did not point at Judas. They did not even look in his direction. They looked at Jesus and—in full terror—they asked him, every one for himself, "Is it I, Lord?"

7

PONTIUS PILATE
Keeper of Law and Order

John 18:28 to 19:22

Law and order are at a low ebb in our country today. Street crime is rampant in our large cities. White-collar crime, though far less advertised, seems at an all-time high —and its yield is a thousand times higher than the lowly "take" of muggers and purse snatchers. The cry for law and order speaks to our personal anxieties as well as to our commitment to civil liberties, for majorities as well as for minorities—because personal freedom cannot survive without law and order. At the same time, we dare not forget that Jesus was put to death lawfully, so that order might be preserved.

Keeper of Law and Order

Who really was this Pontius Pilate, governor of the Roman provinces of Judea, Samaria, and Idumea from the years 26 to 36 of what later came to be known as the Christian era? What kind of man was Pilate? What was he like as a keeper of law and order?

First published in 1972 by Cathedral Publishers, Royal Oak, Michigan. Reprinted by permission.

From non-Christian sources we learn three things about Pilate's administration, all of which indict him at least for insensitivity to the condition and feelings of his subjects. At one time he triggered a riot in Jerusalem by having his army parade through the city bearing the Imperial standards, which displayed the image, the physical likeness, of the emperor. Pilate knew, or should have known, that the display of any image of a god—for the emperor was supposed to be a god—would cause blood to flow in the streets. Blood flowed, because the Jews took seriously the commandment that forbade them to bow down to idols.

Another time, Pilate confiscated money from the Temple treasury in order to build a new aqueduct for Jerusalem. Even if the aqueduct was needed to relieve a distressing water shortage, the question remains: did Pilate have to finance the project by such a heavy-handed, indeed blasphemous act?

The third time Pilate showed himself in the fullness of his insensitivity, his mistake cost him his job. A number of unarmed Samaritans, harmless religious fanatics, had begun to dig around in their sacred mountain in search of some golden vessels that Moses had supposedly buried there. Smelling revolution, Pilate had them slaughtered, no doubt on the conviction that the only good Samaritan is a dead Samaritan. But Roman law applied even to governors. Upon news of the slaughter, Pilate was recalled to Rome and subsequently banished.

We might assume that anything we learn about Pilate from Christian sources, from our deeply prejudiced Gospels, would be highly unfavorable to him. Surprisingly, this is not so. In John's Gospel, Pilate appears as a near-hero, while the Jewish authorities and the Jewish street

mob come off as the only villains. But even in the Synop-
tic Gospels, Pilate cuts a pretty fair figure.

For instance, by asking Jesus the question, "Are you
the King of the Jews?" Pilate in effect announces that this
is a fresh trial. It suggests that he has not prejudged Jesus
in spite of the sentence passed on him by Caiaphas' court.

Again, Pilate expresses his belief in the innocence of
Jesus clearly and repeatedly. Luke has him saying "I find
no crime in this man." And Matthew and Mark join Luke
in quoting Pilate's plea to the shouting mob, "Why, what
evil has he done?"

At last, when it is obvious that reasoning cannot quiet
the mob, Pilate makes one more attempt. He offers the
mob a choice: Jesus or Barabbas. But Caiaphas and his
party have done their homework. They have enlisted a
claque and paid them handsomely. There is no doubt as
to the outcome: Barabbas is "the people's choice."

So we read: "When Pilate saw that he was gaining
nothing, but rather that a riot was beginning, he took
water and washed his hands before the crowd, saying, 'I
am innocent of this man's blood; see to it yourselves.' "
(Matt. 27:24.) And with this gesture, Pilate earned himself
a unique place in Christian history; he is the only pagan
enshrined in a Christian creed. For as long as there are
Christians on earth, they will fix their Lord's time and
place in history with reference to Pontius Pilate, keeper of
law and order, declaring that Jesus Christ "suffered under
Pontius Pilate; was crucified, dead, and buried. . . ."

Symbol of Government

So much, then, for Pilate, keeper of law and order.
What about Pilate, symbol of government?

For the Jews of Jesus' day, Pilate was more than a governor, he was a symbol. He was a symbol of Rome, of the Empire, of a government worldwide in scope, amazingly efficient, and—for its day—remarkably humane. Indeed, Imperial Rome came close to being what the United States so proudly proclaims itself to be: a government "of laws, not of men," a system where justice is vested not in individuals but in institutions designed to transcend the frailties of individuals.

But if Pilate was a representative symbol of that system, the system was not living up to its claims. There he was, lord over life and death in his provinces, wearing the mantle of supreme constitutional authority, a symbol of both *Vis Romana* (Roman power) and *Pax Romana* (Roman peace). But behind the impersonal majesty of the system and its symbol, there was a weak, paunchy, middle-aged man. Beyond the court docket that read "Jesus, Galilean" hovered the personal agenda of "Pontius Pilate, Roman," with his dread of a riot and/or of a bad report about himself to the emperor. Thus in the end it was not Roman law, that lofty abstraction, but Pontius Pilate, a man with political power, who decreed the death of Jesus, a man without political power.

Can any system of government ever succeed in placing law above men? In taking politics out of the administration of justice? In removing the personal equation from governmental decision-making? The ideal is noble and worth striving for. But any sweeping claim of success, whether the claim is made on behalf of the Roman eagle or the American eagle, is open to suspicion.

Of course it is easier to be humane within a good system, and harder to get away with rank evil. But as long as the governing is done by human beings, decisions will always be influenced by "politics." Politics inevitably involves collective self-interest and all the self-seeking personal agendas that ride in its wake. Thus the system itself will appear wonderful to some, a mixed bag of goods to others, and, to still others, a sham-ridden engine of oppression.

In other words, whether you experience the government of Rome, or the government of the United States, as a system of justice or a system of injustice, depends very much on who you are: Roman citizen or provincial subject; anglo or latino; patrician or plebeian; a taxpayer living on wages or a nontaxpayer living on unearned income; master or slave; man or woman.

Even Paul's famous advice in Romans 13, the chapter that recommends uncritical submission to governmental authority, has to be read in this light. When Paul was expressing his views on government and on the responsibilities of citizenship for Christians, he was inevitably reflecting his personal experience and beliefs. For example, Paul clearly and honestly expected the return of the Lord in his lifetime. Thus, even if he had felt like inciting to revolution against the Roman "establishment," he would have given up the notion as hopeless—if only for lack of time!

But Paul had little cause to feel dissatisfied with Rome. While he was a Jew, he was also a freeborn Roman citizen, and he valued his citizenship. In the course of his travels, he could hardly help being thankful to the Imperial government for the vast network of good roads it had created and for the high degree of personal safety on these roads.

Whenever Paul got into trouble with his fellow Jews,

he unhesitatingly appealed to Roman justice and, eventually, to Rome's supreme court, to Caesar. For Paul had it good under Roman rule. It was easy for him to write to the Christians in Rome: "Let every person be subject to the governing authorities. For there is no authority except from God, and those that exist have been instituted by God." (Rom. 13:1.)

Unfortunately, ironically, and suggestively, by the time Paul's case came up in Caesar's court, the throne was occupied by a different Caesar! The system had not changed, but the man who sat at the top of the system's pyramid had decided to use the system differently. Unlike his predecessor, this new Caesar defined Paul and his fellow Christians as subversives, enemies of the state, firebrands—both figuratively and literally!

The new Caesar's name was Nero. He too was for law and order. He too was a symbol, the supreme symbol, of Roman government. But under him, Paul no longer had it good. Unless you believe that Paul enjoyed being crucified. Head down. . . .

Pontius Pilate knew that Jesus was innocent but he chose to use the law to accommodate his personal self-interest and the group self-interest of the populace. Barabbas at large presented a lesser danger than Jesus did. Was Pilate a complete villain then? No. He was a weak, paunchy, middle-aged man; and, unknown to himself, he was a perceptive, nearly clairvoyant man. How so? Because the main charge against Jesus was that he was a revolutionary; and, in a strange, unsuspected way, that charge was true!

What did Jesus say?

He said, "Render therefore to Caesar the things that are Caesar's, and to God the things that are God's." (Matt. 22:21.)

But what does this say, really say?

If God and Caesar are alike, if they are on a par, it says nothing. If our loyalty to God is not supposed to exceed our loyalty to Caesar, Jesus' words are harmless, his statement safe—like Romans 13.

But if Jesus really meant what he was saying throughout his public ministry about God's total claim on our lives, about God's demand for our total loyalty, then "Render to Caesar" is a clarion call to criticism. It is a call to criticize any government, any system, that claims to be above criticism, even if the claim is made, as it usually is, in the name of law and order, or national security, or patriotism.

Thus Pontius Pilate, keeper of law and order, symbol of government, reminds us that human authorities are human; that they can be inhuman; and that sometimes they cannot be rehumanized except by drastic means.

Pilate also reminds us that history's judgments, God's judgments, often differ from the judgments of men. What Pilate composed, in mockery of Caiaphas and of the howling mob, proved true—and then some. The inscription on the cross, JESUS OF NAZARETH, THE KING OF THE JEWS, turned out to be a feeble understatement. The strange, gentle "king" whose life Pilate could have saved but did not have the courage to save, *was* the Messiah, the Savior of all who would seek and accept salvation through him. In fact, we would know nothing about Pilate—he would have gone down history's fathomless drain—were it not for Jesus who "suffered under Pontius

Pilate, was crucified, dead, and buried, . . . descended into hell," and, "on the third day, rose again from the dead"—still under Pontius Pilate. But then he was no longer "under" anyone, for God had placed all things under his feet!

8

BARABBAS

The Man Who Knew
that Jesus Died for Him

Matthew 27:15–26

Among the many participants in the Passion of our Lord,
none is more intriguing than Barabbas. This man was
given his life so that Jesus might be put to death, thus he
was the only man who knew, for a literal fact, that Jesus
died for him.

There is very little we know about Barabbas. While
all four Evangelists mention him, they tell us next to nothing about his background and absolutely nothing about
his life after his pardon. Matthew is content to call him
"a notorious prisoner" (Matt. 27:16). Mark and Luke
credit him with having been the leader, or at least an
important participant in a recent insurrection—a rebel and
a murderer (Mark 15:7 and Luke 23:19). John merely
writes: "Now Barabbas was a robber" (John 18:40). It is
most likely that Barabbas was a Zealot—like Simon and
probably Judas: a member of that small, fanatical sect of
patriotic Jews whose periodic revolts against the Romans
were unfailingly rewarded with long rows of crosses.

Copyright 1962 Christian Century Foundation. Reprinted by permission
from the April 1962 issue of *The Pulpit* (now *The Christian Ministry*).

The Man as Symbol

Although we know little about Barabbas the man, we can at least find in the story of Barabbas the Zealot the symbols of a few ageless truths.

For one thing, Barabbas stands as a symbol of the frustration of the little man in the face of Big Power, structured and entrenched. This frustration is dramatically apparent in any mass society, ancient or modern. The major difference is that, in ancient times, the ruler or ruling class could afford to be more honest. Caesar did not have to justify himself before the mass of the people, most of whom were slaves anyway. Today's Caesars, be they individuals or ruling cliques, are different. They take pains to justify themselves, on television, at the bar of something called public opinion. "The national interest calls for . . . !" "There is treason among us!" "The welfare of our nation demands costly sacrifices from every loyal citizen!" Such are the slogans of persuasion that are being used today to keep the little man fired up, and in line. No wonder that from time to time the little man goes berserk and starts hurling rocks at tanks, as in Czechoslovakia in 1968, or committing single acts of foredoomed rebellion, as in the Republic of South Africa today.

Yes, Barabbas is as frustrated as ever. Occasionally he lashes out against the powers that be in blind fury. But his defeat is sure because he has nothing to offer—except violence.

Barabbas the Zealot also stands as a symbol of violence and of the self-defeating character of violence.

We claim to be a peace-loving, peace-seeking nation, but every seventh person in our labor force depends on "national defense" for a living, and nearly half of our Federal income tax dollars are spent on "defense." We have the capacity to exterminate the whole human race, ourselves included, many times over within a couple of hours, though no one knows how a human being can be killed more than once! Meanwhile our disarmament talks lag and drag. This is partly because we are dealing with other muscle-bound, violence-trusting nations. But it is largely because we cannot imagine what would happen to our economy if peace should "break out." Thus, without meaning to engage in violence, we follow the course of our thoughtless, largely subconscious commitment to violence, which makes most of our peace talk strangely unreal.

Perhaps Barabbas had been in the audience when Jesus warned his hearers concerning the fate of those who take up the sword. Perhaps he had heard the Master's graphic words about turning the other cheek and going the second mile. If he had, it apparently did not affect him. Barabbas was too deeply committed to violence; and the result of his ultimate recourse to violence is a matter of record as well as a telling testimony to the awful futility of violence.

Barabbas the Zealot also stands as a symbol of the politics of justice. It is idle to pretend, even in our democracy, that the administration of justice towers majestically above the flux of political life. Remember: it was the Supreme Court, in 1896, which confirmed "separate but equal" as a proper adjustment between the white and black races; it was the same Supreme Court, in 1954, which threw out "separate but equal" as a doctrine unworthy of a democracy. The difference between the two rulings was essentially political. In 1896, the United States was simply not ready, politically, for the concept of justice embodied in the 1954 ruling.

In the case of Barabbas, we encounter the politics of justice in simpler, cruder form. Pilate, at least according to John, kept trying to set Jesus free, but the mob, incited by the Jewish leaders, threatened him with political reprisals. "If you release this man," they shouted, "you are not Caesar's friend; every one who makes himself a king sets himself against Caesar!" (John 19:12.) Whereupon Pilate's conscience buckled and collapsed. Clearly, the politics of justice called for the release of Barabbas.

For Me

Thus Barabbas illuminates, symbolically, certain perennial features of the human tragicomedy: the frustration of the little man in the face of Big Power; the constant popularity and unfailing futility of violence; and the influence of politics on the administration of justice.

But the central message Barabbas has for us concerns the doctrine of the atonement, the interpretation of Christ's sacrificial death. Barabbas was, after all, the first man who could truly say, and perhaps did say: "Jesus died for me."

To be sure, Barabbas' ability to interpret the death of the Nazarene was rather limited. All he really knew was that Jesus was dying *in his place.* How would this knowledge affect Barabbas? Quite likely he would hail it as a stroke of unbelievably good luck. He would thank his lucky stars, literally. At the same time, being as egotistical as he was superstitious, Barabbas would find in his good luck a vindication of himself and of his cause, the Zealots' cause. "God must have big plans for me after all," he would mutter. "Next time we strike, we shall win; and then we shall wipe out all the Romans and all their Jewish hangers-on!"

There is, however, the one chance in a thousand that Barabbas perceived a more profound meaning in the death of the Nazarene. Suppose he had known Jesus and had heard him preach. Barabbas might conceivably conclude that Jesus was dying not just in his place but somehow *for his sake.* In that case, the substitution of Jesus-bar-Joseph for Jesus-bar-Abbas might be calculated to have an important effect upon the latter. If Jesus was giving his life for Barabbas, just for him, it might behoove Barabbas to acknowledge and respond to the gift. However, even if Barabbas was able to make the long leap from "in my place" to "for my sake," he still faced the stubborn question, "What can I do about it?" And, historically speaking, there was nothing he could do.

Barabbas could not do anything to save Jesus. As an expert in guerrilla warfare, he knew that any last-minute rallying of forces to stage an escape for Jesus was out of the question.

Nor could Barabbas do anything to repay Jesus. He had nothing to offer to the Man who was dying in his place as well as—somehow—for his sake: nothing, except *gratitude.*

With this insight, the awareness that all he could do in response to Christ's saving death was to be thankful to him, Barabbas would have found himself on the threshold of historic Christian doctrine. Alas! This doctrine—that we can do nothing in response to our Lord's gift of his life except to be thankful—would not have been any more popular with Barabbas than it is with us. Who *likes* to be thankful? And helplessly thankful, to boot?

To go one step further, another very long step: what if Barabbas had managed to connect the death of Jesus with his, Barabbas', sins? What if, by an onrush of illumination, he had been enabled to discover the element of *atonement* in the accident of substitution? A far more profound intuition, to be sure, but, for that very reason, far more dangerous, not only for the historical Barabbas, who is quite unlikely to have plumbed such depths, but for us!

In his "For the Time Being: A Christmas Oratorio" W. H. Auden warns against this danger with biting wit. Speaking through King Herod, Auden "foresees" all the mischief that will surely arise when all kinds of people begin to say "Christ died for my sins," or words to that effect. What will be the result of this belief? "Justice," Herod says, "will be replaced by Pity as the cardinal human virtue, and all fear of retribution will vanish. Every cornerboy will congratulate himself: 'I'm such a sinner that God had to come down in person to save me. I must be a devil of a fellow.' Every crook will argue: 'I like committing crimes. God likes forgiving them. Really the world is admirably arranged.' " (*Collected Longer Poems*, p. 189; Random House, 1969.)

Poetic license? Open any collection of "gospel hymns" and see how many of them fairly crawl with shameless pride! Where is the boundary between confessing and bragging? Little Jack Horner, of Christmas pie fame, was at least normal enough to be proud of "what a *good* boy" he was. But this "Christ died for me" piety exhibits an inverted Little Jack Horner complex, to the happy refrain, "What a *bad* boy am I." Strange are the ways of man's cardinal sin, pride!

Yes, Barabbas could easily become the symbol and

the bulwark of that smug, self-centered piety which some of our American forebears of the late nineteenth century bequeathed to us. Adherents of this piety take strange pride in professing to be the meanest of sinners. They also profess that all the complex ills of the world would soon be cured if we could only persuade everybody to say, in just those words—no embroidery, please—"Christ died for my sins." Instantly, there would be peace on earth as well as standing room only in heaven. Such diverse and upsetting problems as street crime, inflation, the energy shortage, the Middle East stalemate, the education of gifted youngsters, the care of neglected oldsters, would automatically be resolved in a flood of pious goodwill! Farfetched? If you think so, I sentence you to one six-hour stretch of radio listening—any Sunday from 6:00 A.M. to 12:00 noon!

For Us

What antidote is there for this flagrant misreading and distortion of God's saving act in Jesus Christ? How can we protect Barabbas from being used as the symbol of a piety wholly unworthy of an honest rogue like him? How can we prevent the doctrine of the atonement, that bedrock of historic Christian faith, from being monopolized by the self-centered, the standpatters, the socially insensitive? Perhaps the best we can do is to steep our own minds in the church's faith in order to understand, really to understand, the meaning of the Atonement. Then, when anyone says to us, whether sweetly or belligerently, "Christ died *for me*," we will be able to counter, "Christ died *for us*"! And this little difference, this replacement of a singular with a plural, gives us the basic clue for our preaching, our conversation, and our striving for a meaningful, practical obedience to our Master and Savior.

Let us illustrate this difference between "for me" and "for us" in terms of Barabbas.

We have said that Barabbas stands as a symbol of the little man, helpless in the face of Big Power. A "for me" doctrine offers consolation mainly in the hereafter: hence Karl Marx's jibe about religion as the "opiate of the people." But if we see the death of Jesus Christ not as a private transaction between God and "this sinner" but as a conclusive revelation of God's redemptive love for all humans, we will be seized by what the Quakers call a "concern." Rather than just offering cups of cold water to the parched little men and women of the world, we will begin to make common cause with them, just as our Lord made common cause with those whom the Sadducees and the Pharisees regarded as worthless outcasts. In the grip of a "for us" vision of the cross, we will seek and find ways to identify and challenge the structures of power, the entrenched vested interests, both governmental and private, which keep little people oppressed.

We have said that Barabbas stands as a symbol of violence and of the awful futility of violence. A "for me" doctrine of the atonement has often given individual Christians impressive courage in the face of torture and even death. But martyrdom without a program may be just so much holy waste. Only a "for us" vision of the cross offers at least the outlines of a program of nonviolence. If we see the death of our Lord not as a private transaction between God and "this sinner" but as a demonstration of the victory of divine nonviolence, our witness for peace will take wing. We will be able to insist, more persuasively than ever, that our unexamined commitment to violence is suicidal; that there must be more daring nonviolent alternatives to solving problems between nations than diplomatic tough talk from a position of bomb-laden strength; and that, in the eyes of our Creator and Redeemer God, our careless dance on the brink of mankind's mass grave must appear as the ultimate blasphemy.

Finally, we have said that Barabbas stands as a symbol of the politics of justice, of the fateful influence of politics on the shaping and administration of justice. A "for me" doctrine of the atonement has nothing to offer at this point except resignation and self-righteous abstention—under the old, tattered banner of "Politics Is Dirty." If, however, we see the death of Jesus Christ not as a private transaction between God and "this sinner" but as an amazing, paradoxical vindication of divine justice, our understanding of politics will be different. Captured by a "for us" vision of the cross, we will accept this world and its ways with mature realism, because it was this world which "God so loved that he gave his only Son." And in this world, politics can be an instrument of justice and mercy just as readily as it can corrupt justice and mercy.

Thus, rather than abstaining from politics and so adding to its corruptness by our self-righteousness and irrelevance, we will be active in politics, beginning close to home where our influence is likely to be greatest; and we will do so because, in this organization age, all major problems that affect the weal or woe of persons sooner or later have to be addressed politically.

Yes, the justice of God and the mercy of God revealed at Calvary command that we engage in politics: to help the Supreme Court hew to its 1954 form rather than have it relapse into its 1896 frame of mind; to safeguard civil liberties at home while creatively opposing fascist and communist powers; and to prevent the church of Jesus Christ from ever becoming, through intimidation or official favor, a tame chaplain either to the *status quo* or to mindless revolution.

The choice is ours, and it lies between that singular and that plural. If Christ died just "for me," he might as well have given his life just for Barabbas, and Barabbas himself would hardly have known what to make of the gift. But if Christ died "for us," for all of us as well as for each of us, including Barabbas, and we let his Spirit plant the meaning of this claim deep in our minds and wills, then God may indeed have some redemptive use for us.

9

THE MAN AT JESUS' RIGHT
Accomplice in the Scandal of the Gospel

Luke 23:39–43

The Gospels are unanimous in reporting that Jesus was not crucified alone. Two other men were being executed with him. We do not know how the crosses were positioned. We simply cannot imagine that the centurion, one of those decent men who was "only carrying out orders," would place Jesus anywhere except at the center. Whether he already had Pilate's order to place the inscription JESUS OF NAZARETH, THE KING OF THE JEWS on Jesus' cross or whether that order arrived later, the Nazarene *belonged* at the center, because he was different. The two others were common criminals; he was at least uncommon.

According to Luke as well as the apocryphal Gospel of Peter, there was a difference between those two robbers; not necessarily in their crimes but in their behavior while in the throes of death. One maintained a brave, profane bluster to the end. The other responded differently and, in so doing, became an unwitting accomplice in the scandal of the gospel. For that reason, he is always pictured at Jesus' right.

The Scandal of Jesus

Why "scandal"? Because the word, once we recall its pristine Greek meaning, is strangely fitting. Scandal means "stumbling block." You walk along, secure and smug, on familiar ground. Suddenly something catches your foot, something hard and bruising. You trip, you curse, and you pick yourself up with your dignity damaged, your face bloodied, your clothing dirtied. Something unnoticed, unexpected, has shattered your composure. You will never again trust your step with the same self-assured confidence. You will never be quite the same again.

The whole life of Jesus had been a scandal.

People walked along, secure and smug about the Sabbath and its time-hallowed use. Suddenly they tripped. Jesus had rolled a rock in their path, a rock marked "The Sabbath was made for man." The Sabbath would never be the same again.

People walked along, secure and smug in their knowledge of neighbor and enemy. They knew who their enemies were and how they felt about them. Suddenly, crash! Jesus had rolled another rock in their path, a rock marked "Love your enemies." Never again would it be quite so simple to love the neighbor or to hate the enemy or even to tell the two apart.

And so it went throughout Jesus' ministry. The disciples felt called upon to plead, to explain, to apologize for their Master, though he never asked them to do anything of the sort. With commendable loyalty tinged with arrogance, they wanted to defend Jesus against the hostility that his unconventional conduct was generating everywhere. But all the while they were themselves shocked, perplexed, scandalized. The Messiah, *if* he really was the Messiah, was not supposed to say such things, to do such things. And yet, most of them believed most of the time that he *was* the Messiah.

But the crucifixion, Jesus' reward for the capital crime of blasphemy, was too much. This was a rock so large, so bruising that even the disciples could neither take it in their stride nor remove it from the path of others. When Jesus hung on that cross, his veins bulging with the strain of his own half-dead weight, his blood draining from his broken body, his lips swollen and barely moving for lack of moisture, there was not one who did not stumble. No one could possibly have perceived in that pitiful failure anything except a pitiful failure. The scandal of his life was being compounded by the scandal of his death. Soon it would be over. Tomorrow would be another day. The day after tomorrow he would be forgotten.

The Scandal of the Man on the Right

Even while dying on the cross, Jesus managed to add to the scandal of his life by saying to the man at his right, "Today you will be with me in Paradise."

The words were scandalous, first of all, because of the man to whom they were addressed. We know nothing about the man except that he had been a robber—more likely a highwayman than an urban pickpocket. There is no hint that he was even a Zealot, a member of that Jewish band of "Robin Hoods" who robbed—and often murdered—the rich but shared the spoils with the poor: desperate "freedom fighters" against Roman oppression. No, this man was most likely a garden-variety criminal.

From his words to Jesus, we may infer that he was a shade more human than the robber who was hanging at Jesus' left. Dorothy Sayers, in her radio plays based on the life of our Lord, speculates that the man at Jesus' left was just a "plain brute, foul-mouthed and vindictive," whereas the man at Jesus' right had "the more engaging qualities of the 18th-century bully. He would adorn a Hogarth print of a Tyburn hanging." (Dorothy L. Sayers, *The Man Born to Be King,* p. 283; Wm. B. Eerdmans Publishing Company, 1943.) In any case, though, it would be too late for this man. What good are a few kind words, or even a full-scale conversion, in Technicolor and Panavision, at the end of a life of murder and plunder? Ever since the Emperor Constantine's calculatedly postponed deathbed conversion, such conversions have been viewed with skepticism and scorn. Should it make any difference that this man was dying on a vertical "bed"?

Moreover, it is not at all clear whether the man's words, "Jesus, remember me when you come into your kingdom" (Luke 23:42) are in effect words of faith or merely words of charity. Sayers suggests that they are "exactly what one would say to please and humor some one who imagined that he was Napoleon." True, our dying Lord seemed pleased. Perhaps he felt that charity might suffice when it is too late for faith. But the people around the cross, including the disciples, were surely not pleased. Indeed, they were scandalized —once more.

The words of Jesus were also scandalous because of their apparent presumptuousness. Here was a wretched man who had wronged society and admitted as much, and whom society, by due process of law, had condemned to death. To this wretch, a fellow wretch now offers a royal pardon! "Today you will be with me in Paradise." (Luke 23:43.) What colossal presumption!

Paradise meant, literally, a well-watered garden, a park. The Garden of Eden was a paradise. In a water-poor country like Palestine, it was plausible that one of the favorite images of heaven should be a luxuriant park. The image reappears in the Apocalypse, where the Holy City is portrayed with the river of life flowing through it, the river of life on whose bank stands the tree of life whose leaves are "for the healing of the nations" (Rev. 22:1–2).

But the scandal of Jesus' words was not just that he was promising this criminal both pardon and paradise but that he was putting himself in paradise. Indeed he was redefining paradise—not as a place but as his company! For that is what Jesus is saying in effect: "Today you will be in Paradise, because you will be with me!" The statement carries an echo from his parting words to the disciples: "I go to prepare a place for you . . . that where I am you may be also" (John 14:3). The disciples had frequently experienced intimations of heaven in the company of the Master. While they had not mustered the courage to die with him, they longed to be reunited with him, at least in that final resurrection in which most Jews believed. But how should they feel upon hearing the dying Master include this outcast, with just an hour or two to live, in his promise of heaven?

There was, furthermore, the scandal of that mysterious and imperious "today." What could anyone make of that? Today was execution day. With luck, if one might speak of luck without grisly irony, the three crucified men might last through the night and into the early hours of the next day. But that would be quibbling. It was plain for any fool to see that "today" did not make sense. Surely this word issued from a mind half-destroyed by the pain of dying.

Even those Jews who believed in resurrection expected that the event would occur ages hence, at a time as far away forward as the six days of creation were far away backward. Thus the words of Jesus "Today you will be with me in Paradise" were morally offensive, not only because of the man to whom they were addressed, and because of their amazing presumptuousness, but also because they were nonsense—theologically speaking.

The Scandal of the Gospel

But the scandal Jesus caused during his ministry and particularly on the cross is the crux of the Christian faith. To be a Christian means to be an accomplice in the scandal of the gospel. In his own unwitting way, the man at Jesus' right became an accomplice of the Master in the scandal of the gospel—and thus a Christian! The Christian life is designed to be a life of rock-rolling, of scandal-mongering. It is our responsibility, as witnesses to God's action in Jesus Christ, to keep rolling rocks across the paths where our neighbors walk, secure and smug in their beliefs and assumptions.

The biggest rock we must roll and keep rolling between people's feet is Jesus Christ himself. It is all summed up in those two words: Jesus, a historic, mortal, dead man. Christ, synonym for Messiah, towering above history, deathless, alive. This rock, this faith-claim, trips up people today as much as it did those who were looking at Jesus of Nazareth dying in the agony and ridicule of the crucifixion. So far as most people are concerned, Jesus never did rise from death. For all they really know, and for all they care, Easter might as well be all eggs and bunnies. And they never will know, they never really will care unless, with God's help, we trip them up so skillfully that they will stumble into the gospel!

When this happens, when a person stumbles over this stumbling block and, by God's grace, finds the Christ in Jesus, then the words of the dying Lord to the man at his right will no longer scandalize.

When we meet the Christ, the Messiah, the Savior, in Jesus of Nazareth, his acceptance and forgiveness of a man whom society has condemned, even to death, will make perfect sense. Jesus had always kept strange company during his brief life. And by his death he created a community whose membership standards were to be strangely different from the prevailing standards of respectability of any society. To that community, whose precise membership is known only to the Lord, a penitent criminal, even in the hour of his death, might find easier access than an impenitent president of a corporation or of a country.

Again, when we have stumbled over Jesus into God's grace and truth, we will no longer be scandalized by Jesus' suggestion that paradise, heaven, means nothing more than being with him—and nothing less. In the perspective of the gospel, death is the gateway to a new life defined and determined by his presence, by everlasting companionship with him and with his own. To anyone who has found God in Jesus, no prospect can be more heavenly.

Finally, when we have met the Christ in Jesus, when we have stumbled over Jesus into God's truth and grace, we will no longer be put off by that "today." Our present experience of a fixed and growing number of *yesterdays*, of a swiftly passing, nearly fictitious *today*, and of an uncertain, diminishing number of *tomorrows,* is somehow absurd. It makes no sense, none whatever, apart from the eternal NOW of God. For with God there is only TODAY. God's people are the only true "now generation," sharing with him the life of Jesus Christ, which is not time-bound but free-flowing, full of love and growth.

This is the scandal of the gospel in which we are called to be accomplices, along with that whole motley crew through the ages, which includes the man at Jesus' right—yes, even him. It is the scandal of God's being in Jesus, the scandal of God's failing in Jesus, the scandal of God's triumph through Jesus.

This scandal of the gospel is big enough without our adding to it the scandal of our incomprehension, inconstancy, or ineptness. It is often difficult for non-Christians to distinguish between the human failure of the church (that is, our failure as Christians) and the victorious failure of Jesus on the cross. It is our responsibility to make sure, as sure as we can, that people will not stumble over *us,* but over Jesus Christ, God's own stumbling block.

10

ANANIAS AND SAPPHIRA

Is a Half Commitment Worse than None?

Acts 4:32 to 5:11

Ananias and Sapphira did not live up to their lovely names. Ananias means "Yahweh has been gracious," but Ananias managed to thwart God's grace. Sapphira means "beautiful"; but this Sapphira, whatever she looked like, leaves behind her a monument of hard-to-match spiritual ugliness.

Ananias and Sapphira, husband and wife, died under suspicious circumstances. There should have been a coroner's inquest. Had there been one, however, it would have been a disappointment to sensation seekers. The verdict would have been heart attack or something equally ordinary. No coroner would have known what Luke, the author of Acts, knew: that Ananias and Sapphira had committed suicide by lying—by lying to God.

A Glimpse of Early Church Life

The story of Ananias and Sapphira, despite its primitive harshness, offers a fascinating glimpse of the

Reprinted from *Presbyterian Life,* October 15, 1963. Used by permission of A.D. Publications Incorporated.

life of First Church, Jerusalem.

It appears that the church at Jerusalem functioned, at least for a time, as a commune. "As many as were possessors of lands or houses sold them, and brought the proceeds of what was sold and laid it at the apostles' feet; and distribution was made to each as any had need." (Acts 4:34–35.) Eighteen centuries later, Karl Marx commended the same principle in almost the same words: "From each according to his abilities, to each according to his needs."

But the practice never became general. In the parallel passage, at the end of the second chapter of Acts, a similar statement is followed by the words: "And day by day, attending the temple together and breaking bread in their homes, they partook of food with glad and generous hearts." (Acts 2:46.) In other words, they did not all sell their homes. Rather, those who had more than they needed for their own households gave all their surplus to the church in order to help those who had little or nothing. Then, under the supervision of the apostles, distribution was made "to each as any had need."

Nor was the practice ever compulsory. Had it been compulsory, there would have been no point in singling out Barnabas, Paul's later fellow missionary, for a special tribute because of his generosity. The Internal Revenue Service does not award medals to wealthy citizens for paying a high income tax. It does give them certain recognition when they fail to do so! But in the story, Barnabas is recognized for his liberality while Ananias and Sapphira are immortalized for their hypocrisy. For that was their sin: not that they refused to give when under orders to do so, but that they lied about the size of a gift voluntarily offered.

Peter's words are plain: "Ananias, why has Satan filled your heart to lie to the Holy Spirit and to keep back part of the proceeds of the land? While it remained unsold, did it not remain your own? And after it was sold, was it not at your disposal?" (Acts 5:3–4.) No, Ananias did not have to give anything. Nor, having decided to make a gift, did he have to give so much. But Ananias and Sapphira were hypocrites. They wanted their fellow Christians to think that they had given their all, while playing it safe by stashing some away just in case. They wanted to have their cake and eat it, too.

Beyond their fate, it is a matter of record that even this spontaneous, voluntary Christian "communism" did not work. Hellenists (Greek-speaking Jews) and Hebrews (Aramaic-speaking Jews) did not become angels by becoming Christians but carried over their tensions into the life of the church, limiting the chances of any share-and-share-alike scheme. Many members of First Church, Jerusalem, both Hebrews and Hellenists, also became slipshod in their economic practices because of their hope that the Lord might return any day. In anticipation, some even gave up working and became public charges. It fell to the newly appointed deacons (Acts 6:1–6) to bring some order out of the incipient chaos. But just then the persecution arose that cost one of them—Stephen—his life, and the experiment collapsed.

There is a footnote here, in the failure of early Christian "communism," illustrating why communism leads to tyranny while democracy, that "worst possible form of government," somehow survives and even assures a measure of distributive justice. Communism is the victim of a false doctrine of man—of what has been called the "angelic fallacy." If we were angels, the beautiful ideal of each contributing according to his abilities and each receiving according to his needs might actually work. But we are not angels! We are sinners, steeped in self-seeking. Therefore democracy, which is based on the doctrine of man as sinner, sets itself more modest goals—like the restraint of gross evil, negotiation and arbitration of conflict, and what the British call "muddling through"—and somehow attains most of these goals most of the time.

A Parable on Discipleship

But the dreadful fate of this couple, Ananias and Sapphira, is not likely to sit well with us. For one thing, we are shocked by the cruelty of the punishment. Did their hypocrisy, contemptible as it was, really deserve the death penalty?

Another difficulty of the story is that the "hero" and "heroine" are so thinly sketched and so unattractive that we may find it impossible to identify with them any more than we can readily identify with Peter pronouncing the death sentence over them.

We get the point, but we are not likely to see ourselves in this man or woman. We may readily admit that we are not doing all we could, all we should, to express our commitment to Jesus Christ and his church, but we decline with horror the suggestion that we may in any way resemble *them!* After all, they were conscious, calculating hypocrites! They knew that they had promised everything without meaning to deliver more than a token, while seeking credit for the whole thing!

Let us forget, for the moment, that the story of Ananias and Sapphira revolves around the giving of something material—land, money, anything. Instead, let us treat the story as a parable on discipleship. Perhaps in this way the story will "come home" to us.

When Jesus called people, saying "Follow me!" the call was meant to be understood literally, and the element of sacrifice was obvious. A man could not "follow Jesus" and remain *where* he had been, let alone *what* he had been. But Jesus was present, physically, for only three short years. At his departure, he left his work in the hands of the Apostles. It fell to their lot to translate his demand for total commitment into practical terms. Thus the original call, "Come *unto* me," changed to "Come *into* me"—"into my continuing body, the church." And the specific meaning of total commitment had to be translated from leaving everything and following, literally, in the Master's footsteps, into shaping a Christian life-style in a pagan world —a far more complex assignment!

Even in Jesus' lifetime there had been men and women who saw his works, heard his call, and said "Thanks, but no, thanks!" This should not surprise us. The freedom in which God created us is a fundamental freedom that Jesus never meant to threaten. Jesus did not compel anyone to become his disciple. He did not choose to be irresistible, lest the very stuff and fibre of both creation and redemption be destroyed.

Jesus set forth the claim of God's love and left the decision to Zacchaeus who responded, and to the rich young ruler who did not; to Peter, James, and John who accepted him, and to Nicodemus who did not; to a handful of inconspicuous people who found in him the promised Savior, and to multitudes who did not.

The same freedom prevailed in the early church. The same freedom prevails to this day. We owe a special debt to our Protestant forefathers for recapturing and reaffirming it. Thanks to them, we live in a country where not only freedom *of* religion but freedom *from* religion is guaranteed by law. Thank God, no one in our nation is compelled to become a Christian! However, for anyone who *voluntarily* becomes a Christian, membership in the church is supposed to be as demanding as it was when the Christian church was young. Just read the *membership vows* in use in your church—the vows you took when you "joined" (that weasel word!). Read them as if for the first time. You will find out, perhaps with a shock, that you have in effect "signed away your life"! Nobody forced you, but you did; so now that you have been reminded of, or perhaps have realized for the first time, the full scope of your pledge, what are you going to do about it?

Discipleship and Membership

Jesus Christ has no quarrel with anyone who never promised him anything. Non-Christians are under no condemnation. On the contrary, they are objects of his seeking love. They are also targets of the worldwide outreach of the church as well as of the community outreach of any congregation. Call it evangelism, call it mission, the pervasive purpose of the church is to win everyone to a spontaneous, glad recognition of Jesus as the Christ, God's unique Son and their Master and Savior. However, the non-Christian who, in spite of the best efforts of Christians, continues to respond "Thanks, but no, thanks" does so with his moral and spiritual integrity unimpaired. He makes no promise; he breaks no promise.

By the same token, our Lord has no quarrel with Christians whose faith has deserted them and who therefore renounce an allegiance they are no longer able to profess. A close friend of many years ago recently left the ministry after declaring publicly that he no longer believed. He did not have to do it that way. He could have done it discreetly, and quietly joined the ranks of those hundreds of ex-ministers and ex-priests who are working in secular vocations. But he decided that nothing less than the whole truth would do, and I believe that the Lord himself respects him for it.

Meanwhile, our churches are full of people who once took their membership vows fully intending to keep them (as far as they understood them), but who now should face the facts and do the only right and decent thing, for themselves and for the church of Jesus Christ, and *get out.*

For Jesus has only one quarrel—a serious one—with his disciples. It is a quarrel with members of his church who pretend to be more deeply committed than they really are. Never mind the first intent. Let us assume that, unlike Ananias and Sapphira, we were honest when we took those membership vows, when we pledged our lives to Jesus Christ. What about *now?* Half-kept promises may be more deadly than broken promises, because they encourage and perpetuate self-deception. No, we are not cheating willfully, grossly. We rationalize. We traffic in excuses. We look to fellow Christians and reassure ourselves by the evidence of their "tokenism," their paltry discipleship. We forget that they may be "half-Christians" because of what they see us get away with!

Our commitment to Jesus Christ, through his church, is in the public domain. From the moment we take those vows and become members of the church, we are "marked men"—and women. If we take our bearings from the performance of others in whose lives their professed faith makes little difference, they in turn look to us—and the sorry condition is compounded. This is why the church presents the tragic compromise between what, in God's design, it should be—and what we cause it to be.

Because of our alibis and our complicity in the alibis of others, we, like Ananias and Sapphira, keep lying to God by keeping up the pretense of total commitment—at bargain rates! This silent conspiracy of lying is killing us and killing the church, too. Not physically, of course, but spiritually. Not in one dramatic stroke but on the installment plan. What indeed can God, even God, do with professed disciples, members of his Son's body, who want to have their cake and eat it, too?

11

SAUL OF TARSUS
The Least of the Apostles

Acts 7:54 to 8:3 and 9:1–19; Philippians 3:4b–14

The greatest of the apostles, Saul (who became Paul), referred to himself as "the least of the apostles, unfit to be called an apostle, because I persecuted the church of God" (I Cor. 15:9). His story stands forth as the most spectacular personality change on record. If the primary meaning of "conversion" is "turnabout," which it is, Saul seems in a class by himself, having scored the full 180 degrees.

The story of how Saul became Paul is a glorious story. It is also a frustrating story, not only because of the radical nature of the change but because, in the process, the entire action seems to be God's. God does everything; Saul nothing. Thus any one of us who hopes to change, and longs to change, is likely to be discouraged rather than inspired. "Oh, well," we might say, "I guess I will change if and when God wants to change me. Until then I am stuck with myself."

The story of Saul as Paul tells it, not once but three times, does lead us to believe that he was overpowered by that light and that voice on the Damascus road, without any preparation, without even any desire on his part to change. No wonder we find it difficult to identify with him—as either Saul or Paul. We are naturally skeptical about how much people can really change after a certain age—and some of us peg that age as low as seven, or even three. Our skepticism is grounded in bitter experience with our own periodic attempts at making changes in ourselves. Thus we write off the story of Saul's conversion to Paul as the result of a unique, supernatural intervention, while we continue to mumble guiltily, self-consciously: "What do you expect? People just don't change very much—if at all!"

To Change or Not to Change

But the problem will not leave us alone. On the one hand, we are confirmed reformers. We keep trying to change others for their own good—and, incidentally, for our own benefit or convenience. We just can't see why people continue to behave senselessly or destructively, year in and year out, when we take such loving pains to point out to them what they ought to be doing and what they ought not to be doing! On the other hand, we realize—at least in those rare moments of honesty that surprise us with pain—that we ourselves are not furnishing any shining example for the targets of our reformist nagging. We are as set in our ways as we wish they were not in theirs!

Why this resistance to change when we know so well what is wrong with us, what needs changing?

For one thing, pride gets in the way. We offer our prayers of confession in safe, general terms—about "the things we have done" and "the things we ought not to have done." We seldom illustrate the words from our own experience while saying them. We sing "Just as I am, without one plea," but behind the familiar tune a still more familiar voice whispers: "Don't be silly. You are not so bad. You are really O.K."

Fear, too, gets in the way. There is an element of risk in every attempt at change. It is easier to complain about the obstacles we perceive outside of us than to face the risk of an unknown, largely unpredictable "new deal." The certainty of who we are and what we have is safer than the uncertainty of what we would like to have and what we would like to be. An imperfect husband or wife may be preferred to divorce and loneliness. A dreary job with regular pay may be better than an exciting job with commission only. Our present self, secretly despised but carefully concealed behind a facade of righteousness and rationalization, may be easier to live with than to abandon, even for the promise of a new, greatly improved self.

Jesus himself did not mince words about the radical nature of the change he required of anyone who would follow him. A young man, oppressed by his own charming futility, asked Jesus what he should do to put meaning into his life. Jesus told him to give away everything he had. Nicodemus found out, with dismay, that he must be "born again"—whatever that meant—before he could really live. Baptism, as Jesus himself received it and as the early church practiced it, symbolized the death of the present self and the birth of a wholly new self. No patchwork here; no exchanging of old frills for new frills. The summons is to conversion, to a complete "turnabout." And there is no precise description of what the new life will be like, nor is Jesus guaranteeing anything for that new life—except trouble! No wonder we shy away from the very word "conversion." We want to change. We pray to God to change us. But not too much!

Subliminal Preliminaries

Saul of Tarsus seemed to be the last man to want to change at all. According to his version, the Lord changed him—in spite of himself—by means of a single, unexpected, awesome experience. This is why the story does not "speak" to us: we do not feel either sufficiently evil or sufficiently important to rate such fireworks! So we plod along, wishing God would help us change, taking feeble stabs at changing ourselves and, in growing frustration, redoubling our efforts to change that stubborn wife or husband, those stick-in-the-mud parents, those impossible kids.

But a closer look at the story of Saul of Tarsus may surprise us. Beneath the suddenness and the drama of the experience on the Damascus road, there are signs that the "birth" of Paul from the ashes of Saul was neither as unforeseeable nor as unsought as it might appear.

At first glance, of course, it seemed impossible that there should be any continuity between Saul and Paul, any resemblance between the man he had been and the man he now claimed to be. The change in him was too drastic to be believed. The Jewish authorities, on whose behalf he had gone to Damascus to prosecute and persecute the followers of Jesus, thought he had gone out of his mind. The Christians feared that he was laying a trap for them. In the midst of this confusion, Paul insisted that, yes, he was a new man! Any resemblance between the Saul he had been and the Paul he had become was merely coincidental! Without saying as much, he denied that there had been any prior experience or influence in his life that might help account for his conversion. It was all the result of the blinding light that opened his eyes, of the irresistible voice that gave him his new marching orders. And it took all the wiles of the gentle Ananias to persuade the apprehensive Christians in Damascus to give him a chance to prove himself—and to keep him out of the hands of the Jews.

But there had been signs in Saul's life pointing toward the Damascus road. God had done some preliminary work in Saul, though it might have been entirely "subliminal," without consciousness on Saul's part. Two figures rise up before us: Gamaliel and Stephen.

Gamaliel, one of the greatest Jewish scholars of his century, had been Saul's early teacher and a formative influence for his thinking. It was at Gamaliel's feet that young Saul had learned to love the Law with such passion that he was ready to jail or kill anyone who dared to challenge its authority. However, it was also Gamaliel who taught the hotheaded young Pharisee the rudiments of toleration and compassion.

We do not learn much about Gamaliel from the Scriptures, but we do have on record his intervention on behalf of Peter and the other apostles (Acts 5:21b–42). In this incident, Gamaliel stands out as the voice of reason over hysteria. He said: "If . . . this undertaking is of men, it will fail; but if it is of God, you will not be able to overthrow them. You might even be found opposing God!" His words are remembered to this day as a charter of free speech and of faith both in common sense and in God's wisdom. No student of Gamaliel could be as rigid, as unself-critical as those who studied under lesser masters.

The other figure that emerges is Stephen. Saul, the model Pharisee, had "consented" to Stephen's death by stoning. Stephen had blasphemed. The Law required only two witnesses, and there were dozens. The Law had to be fulfilled. Significantly, Saul did not himself pitch any stones. That would have been beneath the dignity of a scholar. He was content to guard the cloaks of the self-appointed executioners—they had taken off their cloaks so that their arms might swing more freely. (Acts 7:54–8:3.)

Watching Stephen die, Saul had a vision of Jesus, of the living Christ, several days or weeks before setting out on the road toward Damascus. He had not known Jesus during the Master's lifetime. He had no right or reason to expect a personal appearance from the Crucified. But God gave him a glimpse of the risen Lord in the face of Stephen, in the face of a living, dying, triumphant Christian. And this glimpse Saul could not forget.

Before and After

Thus Saul the Pharisee was not without preparation for the change that swallowed up his old self and gave birth to Paul the apostle. Of course, the difference between Saul's purpose and Paul's, between Saul's activity and Paul's, was total. The latter moved in a completely opposite direction from the former. But even this most drastic conversion in Christian history did not destroy the man who experienced it. Saul changed dramatically. But in the change he lost nothing he was not ready to lose, while gaining more than he had ever dreamed of gaining. Consider just three facts about Saul/Paul that demonstrate how really continuous with himself he was, how plausibly Saul the Pharisee melded with Paul the apostle.

First of all, whether as Saul or as Paul, the man was

a human dynamo. It does not detract one whit from his greatness to bear in mind how large a part his short stature must have played in the shaping of his personality. Saul/Paul had the violent energy of a man who finds his body an inadequate vehicle for his spirit. He goaded his reluctant little body ruthlessly to perform beyond its built-in restraints. He drove himself without pity toward mental and spiritual achievement in order to compensate for his physical inadequacy. As Saul the Pharisee, he was fighting a losing battle. He simply could not do enough. His flesh would not be conquered. But as Paul, the slave of Jesus Christ, he won his fight. Small, sick, depleted, Paul found out that the Lord had made His strength perfect in Paul's weakness and that His grace was sufficient for Paul (II Cor. 12:9).

Again, whether as Saul or as Paul, this man had to serve a master. Saul had found his master in the Law of Moses. He was not drafted to go to Damascus: he had volunteered his services. The harder the task, the better he liked it. The more unpopular the assignment, the more eagerly he sought it. The cause of the Law was his cause. In a profound sense, he *was* the Law. But he could never do enough to fulfill the Law—to satisfy himself.

When his new Master claimed him, all this changed. No longer did Paul have to satisfy himself—only his Master, Jesus Christ, a far more merciful Master. The old swagger was gone. No longer on an ego trip, Paul now traveled under someone else's orders. Someone else drove him on, yes, but also loved and upheld him. And Paul spared no effort to urge his converts to look not to him but only to Jesus. When the Corinthian Christians were forming factions and asserting their loyalty, some to Apollos, others to Paul, and still others to Jesus Christ, Paul let loose a volley of wrath which they would not soon forget. "Is Christ divided?" he asked with fierce sarcasm. "Was Paul crucified for you? Or were you baptized in the name of Paul?" (1 Cor. 1:13.) He had given absolute obedience to his first master, the Law, which had failed him. Now he was giving total, nothing-held-back obedience to one in whose service he was learning to "count everything as loss because of the surpassing worth of knowing Christ Jesus" his Lord.

Finally, whether as Saul or as Paul, the man was a missionary. His zeal to persuade people remained the same. As Saul, this zeal had been misdirected. Zeal in the service of the wrong master is dangerous. All manner of evil, including that most monstrous of evils, the Holocaust, has been initiated and carried out by men of zeal. But the right Master can harness and use such zeal for his gracious purposes. The zeal Saul had shown in tearing people away from Jesus Christ became a vast source of power for the winning of men and women to the Master.

What, then, is conversion? What is this drastic change, this new life, which we both desire and dread? It is the same life, our life, under a new Master and with a new goal.

Conversion is an act of God, yes! But we are more likely to let him perform it if we understand that it is not like dying; it is much more like being born into our true birthright. We have overemphasized the discontinuity between Saul and Paul. It is time for us to recognize the continuity—the carry-over into Paul's work as an apostle of all that was best, all that was worth anything, in Saul the Pharisee. Such an understanding may make us more open, or at least less resistant, to the kind of change we so dimly hope for and so readily write off as a pipe dream.

Yes, the change in us—if we give God a chance to change us—will be drastic, but through the process of change, whether lightning quick or strenuously long, I will still be myself, with my own body, mind, and gifts intact; only, I will have a new Master and a new goal in life.

In Saul's case, his first master had been Saul. Furiously active, he was going around in circles because, at the center of his furious activity, there was only himself. Then came the light and the voice, unexpected yet expected, long resisted yet long desired. Into the center of Saul's life came Jesus, and with him came trouble—and glory—until at last Paul was able to write: "I have been crucified with Christ; it is no longer I who live, but Christ who lives in me." (Gal. 2:20.)

In the service of his new Master, Paul found a new goal. Saul's goal had been static: to defend Judaism, to keep the old order, to resist the new. Through Jesus Christ, Paul found a dynamic goal. The Master lifted his horizon. He showed Paul a vision of the world where all human beings would know and accept themselves and one another as children of God, and—beyond this amazing vision—a life without boundaries. It was in glad pursuit of this goal that Paul was able to write, "Forgetting what lies behind and straining forward to what lies ahead, I press on toward the goal for the prize of the upward call of God in Christ Jesus." (Phil. 3:13–14.)

It is true that people do not change very much. They are afraid to. They don't really want to. But we can change. We can let Jesus Christ change us. The change may be drastic: a 180-degree turnabout. But the gains will outnumber the losses infinity to zero.

12

JOHN MARK

The Spoiled Brat
Who Wrote a Gospel

Acts 12:1–12; 13:4–5, 13; 15:36–41

We know very little about the authors of the four Gospels, and much of what we know is negative.

We know, for example, that the John who wrote the Gospel of John was not one of the twelve. He was a later disciple who perhaps got some of his materials from the original John, and who wanted to be linked with the "Beloved Disciple" to enhance the credibility and significance of his Gospel. Hundreds of years before the first copyright laws, this sort of thing was common practice and in no way illegal or even bad form.

We know, likewise, that Matthew was not the publican, also known as Levi, who was one of the twelve. What we know about the evangelist Matthew is purely circumstantial, and very little at that.

We do know a little more about Luke. The autobiographical materials in Luke's "second Gospel"—the Acts of the Apostles—are obviously authentic. So are Paul's references to Luke in several of his epistles. Unfortunately, in spite of his broad exposure as Paul's traveling companion and "beloved physician," Luke also remains a ghost. We do not learn anything about his background, his character, his passions.

Mark alone is an exception—and what an exception! A young copout and dropout, Mark made the comeback of the ages when he wrote the Gospel, or at least the substance of the Gospel, that bears his name. His Gospel is embodied and elaborated in Matthew and Luke. And his Gospel, by way of Mark's hero Simon Peter, brings us closest to Jesus!

Mark's Defection

John Mark was born in Jerusalem, into a good Jewish home, fifteen or so years after the birth of our Lord. This would make him about eighteen at the time of Jesus' death, which would just about fit.

He was born into a fairly well-to-do family. The parental home stood on the southern slope of Mount Zion, in a pleasant residential area that was also, according to tradition, the neighborhood in which Pentecost, the outpouring of the Holy Spirit, occurred.

Mary, John Mark's mother, was one of the earliest disciples of Jesus. The "church" in her house was one of the first, perhaps the first, house church in Jerusalem. This would make Mary's home the "mother church" of the Christian movement. When Peter was imprisoned, shortly after Pentecost, and then miraculously delivered, he went straight to the house of Mary. He knew that his friends would be there, anxious about him, praying for him. Thus Mary figures importantly in the annals of the first Christian church. However, there is no mention of her husband. Most likely she was a widow, in which case John Mark was brought up only by his mother.

John Mark comes on the scene in our Lord's lifetime. The incident occurs in Mark 14:51–52. Even though he does not name himself, scholars are fairly well agreed that the young man who escaped at the time of Jesus' arrest in Gethsemane is the eighteen-year-old future evangelist himself.

All Mark needs to do is to remind his readers of the episode they had no doubt heard about dozens of times: how he followed his hero Peter into the dark garden where the Master had asked his disciples to accompany him; how Judas came, with the soldiers, to arrest Jesus and as many of his followers as they might catch; and how he, John Mark, managed to get away by slipping out of his cloak and fleeing clad only in his tunic.

Hardly a heroic beginning. But the consensus is that John Mark was not yet a Christian but only a hero-worshiper of Simon Peter. In fact, he was most likely Peter's interpreter for Greek-speaking audiences. The burly fisherman, who spoke even Hebrew, or rather Aramaic, with such a guttural Galilean accent that cultivated Judeans made fun of him, could hardly be expected to shine in Greek.

The other major influence in young John Mark's life was his uncle Barnabas, a Jew from Cyprus, who had vouched for Saul of Tarsus before Peter, James, and the rest. Subsequently Barnabas enlisted Saul as the leader of the church's mission to the Gentiles, beginning at Antioch in Syria.

It was at Antioch that Barnabas, with just a touch of nepotism, persuaded Saul, "who is also called Paul," to take along his young nephew, John Mark, to serve as their *hypēretēs,* which is colorlessly translated as "assistant" but really means "errand boy": anything from secretary to valet. Paul was willing to give the youth a chance, so they set out on what came to be known as the

First Missionary Journey. (Acts 13:1–5.)

All went well at the first stop, Barnabas' native Cyprus, where Paul effectively put down the machinations of Bar-Jesus, better known as Elymas the magician. From Cyprus, they crossed back to the mainland that is now Turkey, to the big seaport of Perga in the province of Pamphylia. There a crisis occurred. Paul and Barnabas pushed on, inland, into the mountainous, semicivilized interior while John Mark, hardly old enough to vote, announced: "Count me out: I am going home!" And he did go home, all the way to Jerusalem. (Acts 13:13.)

Mark's Reasons—Maybe

How do we know that Mark's return to Jerusalem was a copout rather than a move agreeable to all? We know it from Acts, ch. 15, where Paul and Barnabas themselves are back in Jerusalem being commissioned for what came to be called the Second Missionary Journey. Barnabas again urges Paul to take his nephew along. But Paul says: "Nothing doing. One defection is enough!" The argument between Barnabas and Paul results in their parting company, presumably forever. Paul takes Silas, while Uncle Barnabas takes along his rejected nephew, John Mark. (Acts 15:36–41.)

How can we account for Mark's copout at Perga, a defection so spectacular that Paul refused to forgive him? There are at least five good guesses which add up to a reasonable probability: young John Mark, future author of Mark's Gospel, was *a spoiled brat!*

Here are the five guesses.

First of all, if John Mark was brought up in a good Jewish home without a father, he was brought up by a

Jewish mother who, quite likely, was a "Jewish mother"!

Secondly, once he became a Christian, John Mark, being Mary's son, no doubt regarded himself as a "Mayflower Christian." A scion of the family in whose home the Christian church was cradled if not born, Mark was bound to have mixed feelings about that prominent latecomer, Paul. Not only had Paul not known Jesus, he had cruelly persecuted Jesus' followers. No doubt John Mark felt an aristocrat's scorn for the latecomer Paul.

Thirdly, if Paul had been easy to work with, John Mark might have managed to control his feelings. Unfortunately Paul possessed a classic "authoritarian personality," and if there was one thing young Mark could not stomach, it was authority. Hero worship, yes! Mark had known Simon Peter from boyhood, and following his hero around became his favorite pastime. Affection, yes! Mark loved his uncle, Barnabas, who had no doubt been a father substitute and early playmate for him. This is why he resented Paul all the more when, at the close of the First Missionary Journey, Paul turned out to be the "senior partner." "Barnabas and Paul" had become "Paul and Barnabas."

But it was most likely the discipline Paul expected that really turned young Mark against him. Paul was not a leader to say "please." Super-strict with himself, he was strict, though just, with his co-workers. And Paul's temper, always a bit short, was put to the sorest test at Perga in Pamphylia. It was there, at least according to a number of scholars, that Paul acquired his "thorn in the flesh" (II Cor. 12: 1–10).

There is no record that Paul did any preaching at Perga. Rather, he and Barnabas pushed inland at once while John Mark went home to mother. Why? Acquainted with the geography and the climate of the area, which have not changed in two thousands years, we may conjecture that Paul caught malaria in swamp-infested Pamphylia. This disease carried a life sentence, subjecting its victims not only to intermittent, racking fever but to recurrent excruciating headaches.

Paul's coming down with malaria would explain not only his "thorn in the flesh" but also why he would insist on leaving Perga at once and moving on, into the mountains, where the roads were often impassable and the people half savage. There at least the air was clean. It would also explain why Mark could no longer take orders from Paul. A forceful boss, shaken by fever and driven half mad by headaches, would be too much for a spoiled, undisciplined youth!

It has been suggested, fourthly, that perhaps Mark copped out because he was having second thoughts about taking the Gospel to non-Jews. A blue-blooded Jew himself, Mark followed the gracious, liberal attitude of his uncle, Barnabas, until they started to run into flak from Gentile audiences. Then, so the conjecture goes, Mark began to experience a change of heart—like the high-minded white liberal after his first encounter with black radicals.

The final conjecture is that Mark had to leave the kitchen because he could not stand the heat. Heckling from fellow Jews in synagogues, skepticism or contempt from Gentiles in marketplaces, and now the prospect of the journey into the hinterland where creature comforts were nil and life was cheap, could easily cause a gifted but badly spoiled young man to quit.

We shall never know in what proportions these reasons were present in John Mark's decision to leave Paul

and Barnabas in Perga and go home to Jerusalem. We
cannot even guess which of them would have been his
main reason. We do know for a fact that Mark copped out
and dropped out. We also know that when Paul and Barnabas were rallying for a second missionary journey at the
home base, in Jerusalem, Paul would not give Mark a
second chance.

Mark's Second Chance

Later Paul did give John Mark a second chance. How
soon, we do not know. All we do know is that, ten years
later, Paul was writing from his prison cell in Rome to the
Christians at Colossae: "Aristarchus my fellow prisoner
greets you, and Mark the cousin of Barnabas (concerning
whom you have received instructions—if he comes to
you, receive him)." (Col. 4:10.)

Also in his letter to Philemon, another "prison epistle," Paul concludes: "Epaphras, my fellow prisoner in
Christ Jesus, sends greetings to you, and so do Mark,
Aristarchus, Demas, and Luke, my fellow workers." (Philemon 23.) In other words, Paul had forgiven John Mark
who had then, at some point, followed Paul to Rome and
was now there, working with him and no doubt caring for
him in prison.

In The First Letter of Peter, still another epistle from
Rome, the writer concludes by telling his readers that their
sister church in Babylon (a Christian code name for Rome)
"sends you greetings; and so does my son Mark." (I Peter
5:13.) Thus, while serving the now reconciled Paul, John
Mark, now in his early forties, was also serving his earliest, his lifelong hero, Peter, who had joined Paul in Rome
and was soon to join him in prison—and in death. It

stands to reason that the letters bearing Peter's name were written by Mark. It is not likely that the Big Fisherman ever learned to wield a stylus!

But while he might not be able to write, Simon Peter could remember. He had memories of Jesus more numerous and more intimate than any man living twenty or thirty years after the death and resurrection of the Lord. And these memories Peter shared, purposefully and sympathetically, with a younger man who had begun his service as a Christian with great flourish, but had badly copped out. The younger man had been preserved for the Lord's work by the deep affection of his hero, Peter, by the unflinching trust of his uncle, Barnabas, and by the eventual forgiveness of his first, stern taskmaster, Paul. Thus we owe the primary source of our knowledge of Jesus' life and work, the Gospel of Mark, to the affection, trust, and forgiveness shown by three middle-aged men to a spoiled brat.

One timeless lesson we can learn from the story of John Mark is that the young have youth on their side, and that those of us who are older, and maybe wiser, must learn to allow for youth. This is something I have been preaching to myself, with mixed success, for a long time. I have never been known for my patience with the less lovable traits of youth, my own children included. I have always found it difficult, in the face of annoyance or disappointment, to allow for youth, for time, for growth.

But as I get older, and I hope wiser, I meet a growing number of truly beautiful persons who used to be insufferable, often destructive teen-agers, or mindless-radical college students or temporary dropouts, at an earlier age, not just from the "rat race" but from the human race. But now they are entirely different: they are responsible, sensitive, compassionate and—the biggest surprise and delight—remarkably patient with *their* children!

What happened here? How did these teen-age copouts, these college dropouts, these young monsters turn out so well? Each case would be different, yet each would also have have much in common with all the others. There would be reasons for the shortcomings of youth, just as there were in John Mark's case. But, as with John Mark, there would be, in every instance, at least one older person —a parent, a relative, a pastor, a teacher, or just a friend —who would have trusted and forgiven the young prodigal not just once but seven times or seventy times seven times.

Yes, I believe that in every case there was at least one older person who loved the spoiled brat through everything—into the beginnings of maturity—and, perhaps, into prominent usefulness to God and mankind.

If Simon Peter, and Barnabas, and even stern, ailing Paul, could put up with an impossible spoiled brat, John Mark, should not we, middle-aged saints, at least *try?*

13

ELYMAS

The Magician Whose Magic Backfired

Acts 13:1–12; 16:16–24; 19:11–20

"It's magic!" you exclaim, with an admiring grin. The word "magic" has a positive ring. It suggests something both charmed and charming. And the word "magician" conjures up a small, nimble, genial fellow with a fast patter and a bag of tricks to delight the child in all of us.

But in the Apostolic Age, some of the fiercest conflicts the church had to fight were with magic and magicians.

Three Examples

What did magic have to offer that so enthralled both Jew and Gentile, and so enraged the apostles? By magic, people were encouraged to seek a shortcut, indeed they were guaranteed a shortcut, to getting whatever they wanted. Since human needs are many and varied and human wants without number, there were nearly as many tricks as there were needs and wants.

For example, people were sick—they hurt—they wanted health. Medicine was in its baby shoes. Mental and emotional disorders were not even medically defined. They were interpreted as demon-possession. Persons accredited, or self-accredited, for healing the mentally and emotionally disturbed were called exorcists. Jesus himself practiced exorcism, and so did Peter and Paul and some of the other leaders in the early church.

In Acts 19:11–20, we read about the sons of a Jewish high priest named Sceva who had watched Paul heal people "in the name of Jesus." They promptly began to adjure evil spirits "by the Jesus whom Paul preaches," since they did not have any idea who this Jesus was! The sons of Sceva were in the healing business as a business, just as so many physicians seem to be today: not out of compassion for suffering human beings but strictly for the money.

Another example of the church confronting the occult arts is the story of the fortune-teller in Acts 16. We all long for security. We are both intrigued and frightened by the future. To lift that veil just an inch, to take the merest peek in order to be able to protect ourselves, is a nearly irresistible temptation. Thus there have always been fortune-tellers, by a great variety of names.

In Acts 16:16–24, Paul is being haunted by a young slave girl who is supposed to be clairvoyant. Clairvoyance, too, was interpreted as demon-possession. When Paul ordered the spirit to leave the girl, she lost her gift and could read the future no more. The owners of the girl were understandably furious. They had been making good money on the girl. So they denounced Paul and his companions as troublemakers, and had them arrested.

Without regard for the slave girl's condition or her alleged gift, the position of the owners was clear. They were not concerned with relieving people's anxiety about the future. They were only interested in relieving them of their money. Thus, when Paul deprived them of a good source of income, they retaliated as meanly as they could.

A third example is the story of Elymas, the self-styled prophet known also as Bar-Jesus ("son of Jesus"—Jesus was a quite common name). Elymas was a Jew attached to the court of Sergius Paulus, the Roman governor of Cyprus at the time of Paul's visit to the island. Elymas and his relationship with Sergius Paulus remind us of another human need that some of us will go to almost any length to satisfy: the need for power.

We do not know much about Governor Sergius Paulus, but it is obvious that no one is likely to go into politics as a career unless power is high on his list of wants. We can assume therefore that Sergius Paulus was preoccupied with power, wanting to hold on to what he had achieved, anxious to move higher up, fearful of rivals.

A cultivated Roman, Sergius Paulus was likely to be skeptical of all religions as well as profoundly superstitious. Thus he kept a private magician, a mini-Rasputin, in the person of Elymas, a *magus* (like the *Magi* in the Christmas story), who claimed to be able to tell by the stars whose political sun was rising or setting.

When Paul came on the scene and Sergius Paulus granted him a hearing, Elymas was deeply upset. If the governor became a follower of Jesus, he might give up his belief in astrology—and Elymas might be out on his ear. So Elymas tried, though apparently in vain, to incite the governor against Paul, who was threatening the magician's vested interests. For Elymas also was out only for himself.

Exploitation

The early Christians opposed magic, and were opposed by all manner of magicians, because the gospel condemns exploitation even more than it condemns superstition. People believe in all sorts of nonsense because they are ignorant or desperate or both. Ignorance and despair are mitigating factors. But what, if anything, can be said in defense of smart people who do not themselves believe in what they are saying or doing, but say it or do it in order to exploit the gullible?

The crime of Elymas was not just that he peddled a baseless pseudoscience but that he used it only for selfish gain: to secure and maintain his hold over the anxious, gullible Roman governor.

The crime of the owners of the slave girl was not just that they let the poor girl wander around making a fool of herself, but that they used her as a kind of circus act. They made good money on her without even giving her a share. It is clear from the story that Paul felt sorry for the girl, and that his wrath was reserved for her owners who ruthlessly exploited her.

And the crime of the sons of Sceva was not that they tried to heal the sick. That in itself would have been praiseworthy. No, the crime of these so-called faith healers was that they did not have faith and they could not heal. To carry on their lucrative exploitation of suffering people, however, they were willing to exploit anything and everything: even the name of Jesus whom they did not know!

The gospel sets us against exploitation in any form. It also sets us against all persons and organizations whose practice it is to cash in, fraudulently, on people's real or fancied needs and wants. It is true, "There's a sucker born every minute." But that can neither alter nor diminish our irreconcilable opposition, as Christians, to the "suckering" of people.

Blasphemy

There is, however, a weightier reason why Christians always have opposed and always will oppose magic and magicians, ancient or modern, slightly absurd or clothed in fashionable garb. It is that magic, essentially, amounts to bending God's will to our will, making God do our bidding.

The worst thing about the sons of Sceva was not that they exploited people by pretending to heal them when they knew nothing about healing. It was that they led people to believe that God could be coerced into healing them.

The worst thing about the owners of the slave girl, and about the slave girl herself, was that they believed in a small god—a god so small that one could look over his shoulder and read, and thus change, the future he had planned: the future that the true God holds sealed within His sovereign wisdom.

And the worst thing about Elymas, the magician of Cyprus, was not his fawning on Sergius Paulus, nor even his scheming against Paul, but his arrogant assumption that, by consulting the stars or performing some other tricks, God's will could be discovered—not in order to be obeyed but in order to be neutralized or changed!

God's Will Is His Own

But wait. Before we begin to feel too comfortably superior to Elymas and his ilk in those remote times and places, let us consider the possibility that they may have brothers and sisters among us today.

Who were all those "false prophets" in the Old Testament—and in the New? They were religious people who, in the name of God, made a mockery of God by claiming that they could change God's will—or that God was on their side and would do only what they let him do! In God's own name, such "prophets" pretended to hold God prisoner by restricting the freedom of his will. In other words, they were magicians!

Again, what was Paul's great quarrel with the Law—the Law of Moses? Paul was distressed, nearly driven to distraction, because he could not perfectly keep the Law. But this is at least as important: before his conversion Paul believed that if any man *could* perfectly keep the Law, he would have God in a box!

The Hebrew religion, built upon the Law of Moses, had degenerated into an endless series of *quid pro quo*'s between God and his chosen people. A "good" Jew could expect prosperity and security to the extent, and *precisely* to the extent, that he was a "good" Jew. Every good deed entitled one to a reward. Every sin bore a price tag in the coin of punishment. There was *no freedom for God!* God could be neither angrier nor more merciful than the Law allowed him to be. In other words, the Law of Moses itself had become magic!

But are we, Christians, free of the taint of magic—of

the temptation to practice magic while calling it faith, Christian faith?

Whenever I try to bribe God by promising him something in return for whatever I want from him, I have hung out my shingle as a magician.

Whenever I pray as if God owed me the answer I want, I have slipped into magic.

Whenever we forget, even if it be in our deepest, most real, most anxious need, that God's will is his own —and that the only right way to pray is to follow every prayer with a sincere "nevertheless not my will, but thine, be done" (Luke 22:42), we become potential suckers for Hare Krishna or Soka Gakkai or the latest American multimillionnaire messiah!

Paul, in his indignation, struck Elymas blind. The blindness, I am sure, was intended as a demonstration, a passing condition—the kind Paul himself had experienced when, as Saul of Tarsus, he was riding toward Damascus.

We know that Saul's blindness gave birth to Paul, the apostle. We do not know whether Elymas learned anything from his blindness or not. We are not told whether the recovery of his sight brought him any new perception of himself, or whether he continued his life work of gulling people as soon as he could see again well enough to pretend to see things in the stars.

What we do know is that magic is not dead and that the gospel embodied in Jesus Christ is our only defense against exploitation and against our own foolishness. The gospel is the good news that God does not need to be either fed or pacified, because he is neither hungry nor angry. The gospel sets us free to search for God's will not because we have any hope of bending his will to ours, but because, out of gratitude for what he has done for us in Jesus Christ, we want to obey his will. The gospel *sets God free*—free to be who he is: the one wholly sovereign God who can do just as he pleases but of whom we need never be afraid!

14

THE SEVEN SONS
OF SCEVA

Failing the Accent Test

Acts 19:1–20

The great city of Ephesus in Asia Minor was a scenic, sprawling, cosmopolitan commercial center. It was also a flea market of religions, where anyone could set up shop and peddle his own gods and cure-alls. Magic and exorcism were major industries in Ephesus.

Into this city came Paul, preaching the gospel of God's love and demonstrating the power of Jesus Christ by healing the sick in his name. Paul attracted a large following. He also aroused the envy of many faith healers who were unable to accomplish what he was accomplishing.

One team of faith healers, the seven sons of a Jewish high priest named Sceva, devised a neat trick. They would borrow the name of Jesus—and Paul's skill in using the name—and practice exorcism with the formula: "I adjure you by the Jesus whom Paul preaches."

It was a clever ploy but it did not work. The first demon they tried to exorcise from its hapless victim "in the name of Jesus whom Paul preaches" responded: "Jesus I know, and Paul I know; but who are you?" (Acts 19:15.) And with that, the demon caused his victim to jump on the seven exorcists and thrash them within an inch of their fakey lives!

Accents

This is a rather crude story, of course. On a different plane, though, it is a parable—a parable on evangelism.

The seven sons of Sceva were phonies. They had the *words* of Christian faith but not the *accent.* So they failed the accent test.

Accents have long been used as a device to test people.

In the Book of Judges, Jephthah and his forces foiled the Ephraimites by challenging everyone with the password "shibboleth." Anyone responding "sibboleth" would be a lisping Ephraimite and would have his head cut off—never to lisp again. (Judg. 12:4–6.)

In the story of our Lord's Passion, there is the episode in which Peter, having smuggled himself into the high priest's court just to be near the Master, is challenged by a servant and betrayed by his guttural Galilean accent.

Jesus himself comments on the revealing nature of accents in his discourse on the good shepherd: "He who enters by the door is the shepherd of the sheep. To him the gatekeeper opens; the sheep hear his voice, and he calls his own sheep by name and leads them out . . . and the sheep follow him, for they know his voice. A stranger they will not follow, but they will flee from him, for they do not know the voice of strangers." (John 10:2–5.)

Against this background, the story about the seven sons of Sceva becomes a parable on evangelism—about the need for genuineness in evangelism.

Ephesus Revisited

Ephesus was a materialistic metropolis. It was also a city of striking contrasts where great wealth coexisted with abysmal poverty. However, rich and poor were united in their adherence to one of mankind's most ancient creeds: "What's in it for me?"

A smorgasbord of religions flourished in Ephesus, but the seemingly infinite variety of sects and cults did have one essential ingredient in common. They were all trying to teach people how to use the gods in order to satisfy their own needs—and greeds. The "What's in it for me?" credo of the marketplace was also the operational creed of the religion industry. The aim was to give people what they wanted rather than to encourage them to seek and obey God's will. The very definition of magic is using God to serve our ends.

There was also in Ephesus a creeping disillusionment with the products of this religious supermarket. Even the goddess Artemis, or Diana, patron saint of the city, no longer satisfied the spiritual needs of the population. While moving from temple to temple, from guru to guru, from fad to fad, people were actually suffering from spiritual malnutrition which only real food can cure. There was then, in Ephesus, a shapeless, unacknowledged longing for the God whose human name is Jesus.

The Respectful Demon

In our story, when read as a parable, the demon represents *people:* restless, confused, disillusioned people; people who need not be mentally ill but are spiritually rudderless; people without Christ.

There is a great deal we can learn from this demon if we accept him as a symbol of the Christless people who constitute the overwhelming majority of the population of the Ephesus where we live.

For example, this demon respects Jesus.

"Jesus I know" is the demon's first word to the seven exorcists. "Jesus I know"—but the word here is better rendered "acknowledge." The demon was saying, "I acknowledge the appeal, the integrity, the power of Jesus of Nazareth."

Respect for the church may be at low ebb, but the figure of Jesus continues to be compelling, inescapable, turning up in strange places. Jesus is celebrated as *Superstar,* a counterculture hero, weak but caring and courageous, a one-man oasis of decency in a desert of official corruption and popular cynicism. Jesus is portrayed as a clown in *Godspell,* a gentle fool but somehow God's Fool, even though God himself is just a vague, unearthly glow. And Jesus turns up in storefronts and at businessmen's luncheons, on surfing beaches and in chapters of Alcoholics Anonymous—wherever people may perceive, no matter how dimly, his gracious availability and unique power.

This demon also respects Paul.

"Jesus I know," he says, "and Paul I know." "Yes, I know Paul, too: I know his mammoth intellect. I know his selfless courage. Above all, I know that Paul practices what he preaches—that his words are of a piece with his life."

And the demon respects Paul's healing ministry.

People disaffected by Christian doctrine or by Chris-

tian worship often retain a great deal of respect for what
genuine Christians are moved to do for others, in practical
ways. A church that serves people as whole persons is
more likely to attract nonbelievers to worship and eventually to faith in Jesus Christ than a church that limits its
concern to "the prayer life and the after-life."

Show Me!

The demon, symbol of all Christless people, respected
Jesus and Paul and the service that Christians rendered to
others as whole persons. In short, he respected genuine
Christianity. On the other hand, the demon had only
contempt for the counterfeit Christianity represented by
the seven sons of Sceva.

Christless, churchless people have no use for evangelism with ulterior motives. This is what makes evangelism
so difficult, especially in the sophisticated urban society of
Ephesus, New York, San Francisco, or Chicago. The
slightest suspicion of ulterior motives—and the door,
which may have been open a crack or two, is slammed
shut again.

Evangelism by ministers suffers from a special handicap, because ministers get paid for being Christians.
Whatever a minister may say to a non-Christian or an
ex-Christian immediately arouses the suspicion: "Is he or
she saying these things for bread-and-butter reasons?"

But laypersons, too, may have an ulterior motive. Not
money to be sure, but a sense of duty. "I really *ought* to be
talking about my faith . . . because I ought to. . . ." Unfortunately, the "ought" motive is also a door-slammer. The
words lack spontaneity, conviction, persuasiveness. The
words may be right but, once again, the accent is wrong.

And the demon, symbol of the world's Christless, church-less people, cannot hear the words for the accent.

The fastest door-slammer, however, is evangelism that springs from a *proxy* faith. That was what the sons of Sceva had—and tried to put to work, for profit. They tried to practice exorcism, to heal the mentally ill, "by the Jesus whom Paul preaches." The phoniness of this gambit should have been obvious to any halfway intelligent demon—or person.

There is a lovely expression in my native Hungarian: "to preen oneself with borrowed feathers." It does not work, but the temptation to keep trying is strong. The minister pleads: "I urge you in the name of the Jesus about whom I learned so much in seminary." The layperson echoes: "I urge you in the name of the Jesus about whom our minister talks so much." But all these "urgings" fail the accent test. They are appeals to authority that do not cut any ice, because the only truly convincing, truly con-victing authority is the authority of personal experience and commitment.

"Jesus I know and Paul I know, but who are you?" That is the question. A proxy faith, lodged in a conven-tional life, cannot persuade anyone to make a deeply per-sonal, highly unconventional commitment. We can only be evangelists, witnesses to God's power to change lives, as we allow him to change us, as his Spirit begins to flow through us into the lives of others, into the life of the world. Meanwhile, we are more likely to be bottlenecks, clogged channels for God's free-flowing grace. We have the words but seldom speak them; and then, when we do, the accent is wrong.

Acquiring the Accent

What can we do?

Suppose that we are not like the seven sons of Sceva —that we are sincere Christians with a faith worth sharing and a genuine desire to share it. How can we acquire both the words and the accent for effective evangelism, for a persuasive witness to God's love revealed in Jesus Christ?

The *words* are not hard to acquire. "I don't know enough" (to be an evangelist) is the poorest of excuses. No one is keeping us from learning more about our faith, about the foundations of Christian faith in the Bible and in the church's teaching. But a single membership training course is not enough. Listening to sermons, even the finest of sermons, is not enough. We cannot become—and re-main—informed Christians, adult Christians, without constant, disciplined reading and continuous sharing with fellow Christians. It is work—hard, lifelong work; but the words required for responsible evangelism, the formal knowledge necessary for intelligent witness, *can* be learned.

The *accent,* too, can be learned—but only by trial and error. The most likely cause of our failure to function as evangelists is not that we are enslaved to ulterior motives, or that we lack a genuine faith, but that *we do not try!* When did you last try? When did you last try to talk with a Christless, churchless friend about your faith—simply, unself-consciously, caringly? What is keeping you from trying?

You may feel that you don't know enough. Perhaps so, but you can try with what you do know—while starting to deepen your knowledge of the faith.

You may feel that you are not "good enough." Of course you are not, but who is? If the apostles had waited until they were good enough, the Christian church would have been stillborn—Pentecost would not have happened!

Or you may feel such a deep respect for the privacy of others that you will not "embarrass" your Christless, churchless friends with even a word about your faith. We Americans do suffer from this obsession. We consider it "bad taste" to discuss religion and politics in personal terms. But what other subjects are as worthy of mature adults, of mature *Christian* adults?

Moreover, you are not really fooling your friends with your "tact." They *know* you are a Christian—or at least claim to be one. They are *expecting* you to talk about what, according to your profession of faith, means just about everything to you! In other words, your failure to speak up may be a betrayal not only of your solemn profession but of their rightful expectations!

"Jesus I know, and Paul I know; but who are you?"

The words will come, as you speak up and as you keep learning more about your faith.

The accent will improve as you keep trying.

The only thing that will not come "naturally" is the *courage* both to get started and to persist.

For that, for that courage, you need supernatural help. But, for that, you know whom to ask.

15

SINNER IN CORINTH

The Man Who Lived
with His Father's Wife

I Corinthians 5

The earliest Christians lived in a pagan, permissive society, just as we do. There was complete religious toleration and a big religious boom, but religion was largely disconnected from morality. Politics was proverbially corrupt. And while no one talked about any "sexual revolution," the sex scene might have been characterized by just two words, "Anything goes!"

Being a Christian in Corinth in the sixth decade of the Christian era demanded, as it does today, that Christians should ask themselves: "How am I supposed to be *different* —as a Christian?" Under Paul's guidance, the Corinthian Christians wrestled with such (to us) familiar questions as "Where is the line to be drawn between Christian and pagan behavior?" "Who is to draw the line—and for whom?" And the guidelines Paul was offering for the sexual conduct of these Christians dramatically illustrate the early church's struggle to develop a Christian lifestyle in a pagan, permissive society.

The Case of the Immoral Man

In I Corinthians 5, we find Paul sharply rebuking the Corinthian Christians for their failure to deal with one of their number—a man who was "living with his father's wife."

The text does not imply incest: surely Paul knew the Greek word for "mother"! Nor is there any implication of adultery. It is most likely that the woman's husband—that is, the father of the "immoral man"—was dead. Nevertheless, Paul affirms in the strongest language that the man's conduct is intolerable, *because he is a Christian.*

Sexual relations between a man and his stepmother were forbidden by Jewish law (Lev. 18:8). They were also illegal under Roman law, even though in Corinth, renowned for its San Francisco-like tolerance, such relations would hardly raise an eyebrow. But Paul is appealing neither to Jewish nor to Roman law. His rebuke is based solely on the ground that the man is a Christian, a member of Christ's body. The church, Paul points out, cannot condone sub-Christian conduct within its ranks.

To correct the situation, Paul orders the man to be excommunicated, placed outside the communion of the church. The wording may strike us as strange and harsh. We no longer talk about delivering people to Satan! But in Paul's thought, the world was under Satan's rule. You left the world to become a Christian. You found refuge in the church from the judgment that God had in store for the world. Thus, excommunicating someone meant simply sending him back into the world, Satan's world, where he had come from in the first place; and Paul makes it clear

that the verdict is designed not for the man's destruction
but to encourage him to repent—and return to the fold.

Bases of Paul's Judgment

On what basis did Paul arrive at his judgment?

For one thing, Paul believed that sex is a trap. He was
sharply aware of the pitfalls of sex, even though he never
singled out sexual misconduct for special censure. Even
his much-quoted indictment of homosexual relations occurs in the context of one of his "catalogues of vices," so
that homosexuality is not being judged more severely
than slander or greed or murder (Rom. 1:24–32). Paul uses
the same approach when dealing with the "immoral
man." He does not claim that this man's sin is any more
awful than the sins of idolatry or blasphemy—or drunk-
enness (I Cor. 5:9–11).

Paul was also convinced that Christians had no business judging non-Christians. He does counsel these new
Christians to keep to themselves as much as possible, but
he knows that they could not avoid contact with non-
Christians even if this were desirable. Paul knew and
shared his Lord's view—that Christians should be "in the
world" even though they were not "of the world." Therefore he encouraged the Corinthian Christians to live a full
life, to live in the midst of life, but not to go around
passing judgment on their pagan neighbors.

On the reverse side of the same coin was Paul's conviction that Christians must judge among themselves—
judge themselves. Paul knew only too well how recently
the Christians in Corinth had themselves been pagans and
how many of them, having heard the gospel, had actually
misheard it. They had heard, correctly, that the gospel

brings freedom from the Law of Moses as well as from the endless rituals of the pagan cults. But many of them misunderstood this proclamation of evangelical liberty as an invitation to libertinism, to license, to "doing what comes naturally"—and unnaturally—especially in the realm of sex! Against this tempting heresy, Paul baldly claims that Christians must maintain—for themselves and among themselves—a much higher, far more exacting standard of sexual conduct than they would be responsible for in any of the pagan religions or even in Judaism.

Questioning Paul's Principles

Paul's principles are clear. No doubt they worked in Corinth in what we now call the first century, because the church survived and grew. But are these principles valid for Christians in the United States, in this closing quarter of the twentieth century?

For example: if Paul perceived sex as a trap, to what extent was his perception colored by his belief in the imminent return of the Lord? And in what degree was his seemingly negative attitude toward sex influenced by the Corinthian scene, specifically? Corinth, after all, was the Empire's headquarters for sordid sex. Towering above the city was the temple of Aphrodite, the goddess of love. Every evening, hundreds of temple "priestesses" (read: prostitutes) would invade the streets of the bustling port, in search of "converts" for their cult. Perhaps Paul's harsh judgment upon the "immoral man" needs to be interpreted against this colorful and repulsive backdrop. Moreover, it has been suggested that Paul's own physical condition had something to do with his attitude toward sex. Maybe his "thorn in the flesh," whether it was malaria or some other chronic ailment, interfered with his own sexuality, giving rise to conscious hostility—from subconscious envy. Or, according to a different conjecture, maybe Paul's sexual drive was so completely sublimated in his missionary work that he had no understanding for normal men and women with normal needs. Such guessing is a game any number can play!

Again, if Paul advocated "separatism" for the Corinthian Christians, could it be that his conviction was colored by his own background as a Pharisee ("Separatist")? If so, is a separatist attitude appropriate for American Christians today? We live at such close quarters in our "global village" that what any of us do affects all of us. More important, what non-Christians do profoundly affects *them* as persons, as human beings. If we believe that God's offer of redemption is designed for all, including those who at the moment ignore or reject his offer, we may find the separatist position unacceptable. What then shall we make of Paul's statement that, as Christians, we have no business judging—that is, meddling with the conduct of—non-Christians?

And what about Paul's conviction that our primary responsibility, as Christians, is to keep ourselves pure, both as individuals and as churches? Are we not rather supposed to be open to people of all sorts, to accept them as they are, to invite them in, rather than keeping them at arm's length? Does not the very pursuit of purity threaten to lead into the pitfall of arrogance, or self-righteousness?

Yes, all these critical questions regarding Paul's principles for a Christian sexual ethic are legitimate. Paul was a child of his time. He was also himself, the former Saul of Tarsus, a Pharisee, transformed into an apostle of Jesus

Christ. But Paul's principles are far more valid today than
they may appear, at first glance, to our self-indulgent
eyes. With a little "translation," they are as relevant for
Christians in twentieth-century "Metropolis, U.S.A." as
they were for Christians in first-century Corinth.

"Sex Is a Trap"

For example, Paul was convinced that sex is a trap.
Well, isn't it? Like everything human, sex is morally am-
biguous, the more achingly so because it is such a fundamental part of our humanity.

Sex can be an expression of everything that is noblest
in us. It can be the crowning act within the most loving,
the most self-giving relationship. Even Paul, none other
than Paul, compared the love of a Christian man and a
Christian woman, in the bond of marriage, to the love of
the Lord for his church! But sex can also be the crudest,
greediest, loneliest thing two persons can do together.

Sex can be a triumphant affirmation of God's love for
us, or a blatant mockery of his love. In an oversexed
society like ours, in our giant cities glutted, Corinth like,
with cheap sex, it behooves Christians to exhibit a critical
difference in sexual behavior—and it is the church's responsibility to clarify and commend that difference. For
where sex is god, Christians must recall the ancient commandment against idolatry: "You shall have no other gods
before me"!

"Christians Must Not Judge Non-Christians"

What about Paul's conviction that Christians have no
business judging non-Christians? Are these words an en-

couragement to indifference? Hardly. Paul is simply saying that we must not apply to non-Christians those stricter standards of conduct which we, as Christians, have voluntarily accepted for ourselves. What would be some of the implications of such a nonjudgmental attitude on the part of Christians toward non-Christians today?

One implication might be that Christians might welcome, even work for, the decriminalization of all manner of sexual behavior among consenting adults. Every sin is not necessarily a crime. The undermanned and underequipped police forces of our crime-ridden cities spend too much time on "victimless crimes," while violent crime goes unpunished. Paul would have Christians bear witness, in word and action, to a "more excellent way" (I Cor. 12:31)—in sexual behavior as well as in all areas of human conduct and relations. He would not enlist the police power of the state to coerce non-Christians into uncomprehending, hypocritical conformity to the standards of Christian sexual morality.

Another implication might bear directly upon today's most widely headlined sexual disorder, homosexuality. The Biblical witness is clear: homosexual *practice* is unconscionable for Christians. However, if the slowly emerging consensus of medicine and psychology can be trusted, homosexuality may be unique in that some homosexuals may actually be "born that way" and, to that extent, helpless about their *feelings.* If this be so, we dare not hold aloof from homosexual non-Christians in self-righteous, blanket judgment. Rather, we should invite them to our churches, individually, just as we invite heterosexual non-Christians. Such a welcome would not approve homosexuality any more than our welcome to greedy businessmen should be construed as an approval of greed. Churches are not designed as clubs for saints. They are supposed to be schools for sinners—and schools are for learning, for growth, for change. As much as he abhorred homosexuality, Paul would agree that we should extend to homosexual sinners the same loving, redemptive concern as we exhibit toward heterosexual sinners. After all, we are custodians of the gospel of God's love, which can effect change in persons even when the chances are, humanly speaking, slim—or nil!

"Christians Must Judge (Among) Themselves"

Consider, finally, Paul's principle that Christians must judge among themselves—that we must judge ourselves. What Paul calls for is in effect a double standard: leniency toward non-Christians, strictness with ourselves. Specifically, Paul demands that the church spell out guidelines for *distinctively Christian behavior*—not just in the area of sex but in every area of life—because, without a visible, significant behavioral difference between Christians and non-Christians, between the church of Jesus Christ and every other organization, the love of God is pilloried and mocked!

The Biblical Christian standard is *marriage:* marriage designed to be lifelong, marriage open to the gift of children. The other Biblical option is *self-control:* the containment of the sexual impulse, whatever its direction, the sublimation of the impulse in socially useful work. All other options violate the standard. Homosexuality does, of course; but so does all casual sex.

This, then, is where the line must be drawn—by the church—for Christians who *are* the church. No one has forced this standard of sexual behavior upon us, because no one has forced us to become Christians—and no one is forced to remain a Christian. The church of Jesus Christ is itself a *community of consenting adults*. We have consented, as adults, voluntarily, to order our lives not by what is legal, nor yet by what is socially acceptable, but by what the Word of God prescribes, or at least permits.

The most graphic indictment of our churches is the seemingly innocuous question that often appears on official forms: "What is your church or club?" Is *that* what our churches have become: clubs? Do we not have anything to distinguish us from "other clubs"? No distinctive discipline? No extra moral demands voluntarily accepted? Nothing to help anyone recognize us at once as disciples of the Lord Jesus Christ? If so, it is time that we closed up shop!

As old-fashioned as it is, we dare not forget the saying "Hate the sin, love the sinner." That is how Paul felt, and acted, toward the "immoral man" in Corinth. He had to judge the man's sin, both for the church's sake and for the man's own sake. But his judgment left the door wide open for the sinner's return—as a forgiven sinner.

"Hate the sin, love the sinner": a very hard thing to do. But Jesus did it, perfectly. Jesus accepted Zacchaeus, who was a crook, but he did not accept crookedness as a moral option, let alone a life-style, for Christians. Jesus accepted the Roman centurion as a person, but he did not accept organized violence as an option for Christians, let alone as a life-style as valid as peacemaking. And Jesus accepted the adulterous woman, just as he would accept anyone guilty of any "sin of the flesh," no matter how grave. But he did not say to the woman, "You are forgiven: carry on!" No, he said, "Neither do I condemn you; go, and do not sin again." Jesus would reject both casual sex and deviant sex, considering them as life-styles not valid for Christians. He would draw the line for Christian sexual conduct to include Christian marriage and self-control, nothing else. In his guidance, to the Corinthian Christians, Paul was only following his Master.

And Paul had nothing to say—in I Corinthians 5—to the stepmother of the "immoral man." Obviously, she was not a Christian. But the man was a Christian, or at least he had been; and Paul made it clear that he could be again.

16

PHILEMON AND ONESIMUS
Two Slaves Set Free

The Epistle to Philemon

During one of his many prison terms, Paul was joined by a runaway slave named Onesimus. In Greek the name means "useful." Onesimus was the property of a man named Philemon who lived in a neighboring city (either Colossae or Laodicea) and was a leader of the church in that city.

In prison Paul befriended Onesimus and converted him. Together they resolved that, in spite of mortal risk, Onesimus should return to his master, Philemon.

The Epistle to Philemon is a covering letter. It is Paul's plea for the master to show compassion for this "useless" slave—a play on Onesimus' name. Paul pleads that, by forgiving Onesimus, Philemon will make it possible for him to begin to live up to his name, to become truly "useful."

The Freeing of Onesimus

What kind of man was this runaway slave, Onesimus?

Apparently, he was a gifted man, in a way. Making a successful escape took brains and courage. There were more slaves than free men in the Roman Empire at that time. The fear of a slave revolt was great. Therefore there were police and stool pigeons everywhere, especially in the slums of the great cities where hiding out was most tempting.

Onesimus was also a desperate man. It required the courage of despair to run away, since the punishment for running away was torture, refined and prolonged torture, with death as the only ultimate escape. A runaway slave therefore might do anything: he was capable of any crime.

Onesimus was a criminal. He had robbed his master, Philemon, when he was making his escape. Why should he not rob him? Why should he not take anything he could from the "master class"? He had no stake in a social order in which he was not being regarded as fully human.

Thus, when Onesimus met Paul, he was quite unfit to bear the name, "useful." He was a useless man, an undistinguished particle of the mass of human waste on which the Empire was built. And Paul was entirely clear-eyed about Onesimus. He did not pretend, even to himself, that Onesimus was anything other than what he was. His suggestion to Philemon, *"If* he has wronged you at all or owes you anything . . ."* is a masterpiece of both graciousness and irony.

But Paul accepts Onesimus. He loves him first, just as he is, because that is how Jesus Christ loves us. Then, when he begins to work with Onesimus, he grows to love him more and more. Before long, he is calling Onesimus his "very heart." He legally assumes his debts. He even wants him back. He expresses the hope that Philemon will not only forgive Onesimus but return him, even though Paul's present plea, for mercy, is so bold that he hardly dares hope for that further gift.

Clearly, Paul helped Onesimus become a new man. It was hard labor. Paul himself describes it as similar to childbearing when he speaks of the runaway slave as "my child, begotten in prison." But the results of Paul's travail were extraordinary. The change in Onesimus was unbelievable. He was born again. He was truly a new man.

In what sense was Onesimus a new man?

He had acquired self-respect—from getting to know Jesus Christ who had given his life in order that slaves, all kinds of slaves, might become free, self-respecting men.

He had also acquired a new brand of courage. This was not the courage of despair that had served him well in enabling him to escape; this was the courage of conviction that now enabled him to return to his master—in the face of torture and death.

And Onesimus had acquired ambition. Up to this point in his life, his sole ambition had been to be *free from* something—from Philemon, from slavery. Now Onesimus possessed the positive ambition to be *free for* something—for the service of that Master whom Paul was serving, freely, thankfully.

Thanks to meeting this Master, through Paul who introduced Onesimus to him, the runaway slave began to grow into his own name. He became potentially useful: to himself, to Philemon, and to Jesus Christ.

The Freeing of Philemon

But Philemon, master of Onesimus and, for all we know, of a number of other slaves, was himself a slave. How can this be so? Because no man is free who holds a fellow human being in bondage. Freedom requires the ability and the opportunity for people to relate to one another as persons, as free agents, openly, spontaneously, givingly. If I treat anyone as a thing, an object rather than a subject, I forfeit part of my own humanity.

Philemon was a good man snugly lodged within an evil system that he was therefore hard put to criticize— or even perceive as evil. Rather, had anyone attacked the institution of slavery within Philemon's hearing, he would no doubt have risen to its defense, conscientiously and cogently. Having experienced the system only at the top, he would not know what it felt like at the bottom.

Philemon would consider slavery essential to the economic stability of the Empire. He would not be able to conceive of any ordering of property and production more efficient than the only one he knew—the one under which he had it good. He would have pointed out to any comer, perhaps correctly, that if all the slaves were freed at once, there would be chaos.

The trouble was that Paul was thrusting his plea at Philemon in *personal* terms. He did not discuss the system as such. He talked about one master, Philemon, and one particular slave, Onesimus. To Philemon, this must have seemed as somehow hitting below the belt!

Philemon would also know, and defend, the social advantages of the institution of slavery. The system enabled him, as a member of the master class, to feel superior to any and all slaves, regardless of what he was like as a man, regardless of what any of them were like as men. Just by being born into the master class, Philemon was assured an unearned, automatic superiority over a portion of the human race. What a powerful ego prop that is!

But now Paul was pointing out to him that, as a Christian, this particular slave, Onesimus, was his *equal*— somehow. Philemon knew that many of the slaves were smarter than many members of his own class. It is possible that Philemon did not know how to read and write—and that among his other chores Onesimus had been serving his master as a scribe. But "social equality" was something else altogether!

Most important, Philemon knew the power of a master over his slaves. Even if we assume that he had been a fair and gentle master (as indeed we may), he would know that there was nothing in Roman law or custom to prevent a master from indulging his every whim with a slave. A master could torment his slaves, physically or mentally. He could make them his sexual playthings. He could take out on them his every impulse, his every frustration. A slave was a "thing" that could neither talk back nor fight back. Moreover, the institution of slavery was the bulwark of political stability—at least of the illusion of stability. Nothing was changing, nothing really could change, as long as the slavery system was intact and functioning to shield and pamper the master class.

Thus Onesimus had been "useful" to Philemon as a "thing." But, in a more profound sense, he had been useless to Philemon, indeed harmful, because slavery is as dehumanizing for the master as it is for the slave. And it was the clear and well-thought-out purpose of Paul to free both Philemon and Onesimus, both master and slave.

Love's Gentle Heat

How did Paul go about it?

For one thing, he did not command Philemon to forgive Onesimus; he appealed to him. Philemon, as a Christian, was subject to apostolic authority. He could refuse an order from Paul only at the risk of his standing in the church. But Paul preferred to proceed in such a way that Philemon could say no, because he wanted Philemon to respond as a free agent, from conscience, rather than under coercion.

But Paul does not content himself with pleading. He mounts a loving stratagem. He enlists the church, Philemon's congregation, in a redemptive plot. By sending carbon copies to Apphia, Philemon's wife, and to Archippus, their pastor, Paul turns on, under Philemon, love's gentle heat. There is always a chance that a woman might have a more tender conscience than a man—though one cannot generalize on this point. There is always a chance that a pastor might have some influence with a layman—though one dare not generalize on this point, either. What Paul knew was that, if Philemon were to muster the courage to do anything as unconventional as forgiving a runaway slave who had also robbed him, he would need "group approval." Without such support, the chances that Philemon would come through were slim indeed.

It is tempting to use Paul's approach in the freeing of Philemon and Onesimus as a formula for dealing with social injustice today. Alas! it cannot be done. The Bible is not a handbook for reform. It is a record, *the* record, of God's dealing with us. Still, Paul's *modus operandi* has much to suggest to us.

For example, Paul's attack upon the slavery system was never announced as an attack—but in the long run it worked. Where all slave revolts were drowned in blood, Paul's way—Christ's way—proved to be the "seed that finally split the rock of slavery" (George A. Buttrick, exposition of "Philemon," *The Interpreter's Bible*, Vol. XI, p. 561; Abingdon Press, 1955.) There is always a wide spectrum of possibilities between pious inaction and foredoomed violence. Paul's method, in this case, might be called peaceful subversion. Working through the church, Paul created a "test case" for undermining the institution of slavery.

But Paul also knew that institutional change without a "change of heart" would always fail in the end. It is true that often institutional change can change hearts. Fair housing laws expose people to new neighbors, feared at first, sometimes violently resisted, but a discovery of common humanity follows the initial tension and a new community is born. Nevertheless, the only lasting guarantee of community is persons with new hearts, persons set free by the gospel to know both themselves and one another as children of God made in his image, persons finding in their voluntary bondage to Jesus Christ their true freedom.

How does the story of Philemon and Onesimus end? We do not know. According to tradition, Philemon sets Onesimus free and Onesimus becomes a leader in the church: bishop of Ephesus and the editor of the earliest collection of Paul's epistles. An extraordinary "happy ending"!

I rather hope, though, that Onesimus did not do quite so spectacularly well. Why? Because Onesimus had a right to be free even if, given his freedom, he chose to stay on with Philemon—to shine Philemon's shoes, run errands for him, wash his chariot.

Onesimus had a right to be free not because he was ready for freedom, nor because he was deserving of freedom, nor yet because he was "bishop material"! He had a right to be free because only as a free man could he be truly Onesimus, truly himself, truly "useful"!

17

SATAN
Our Ancient Foe

Ephesians 6:10–17

Only three short years after his first protest against the
papal church, Luther found himself in the Wartburg, a
fortress where a friendly prince had taken him into pro-
tective custody. There he spent month upon month in
complete seclusion, working on his translation of the
Bible. There, in the strain and loneliness of his work, he
had a vision of the devil—a vision to which he reacted
with characteristic courage and abandon. Tourists can still
see the dent in the wall and the dark stain around it: a
picturesque reminder of the devil's appearance and of the
inkwell that Luther flung at him.

What about the devil? Luther took him seriously.
His writings are full of references to the devil. Luther
interpreted the conflict in which he was playing such a
decisive part as one of the unnumbered battles of the
war between God and Satan. Nowhere in any of his
writings did Luther give more forceful utterance to his
belief in the personal reality and power of the Evil One

than in his great hymn, *"Ein' feste Burg,"* which became
the battle hymn of the Protestant Reformation.

> A mighty fortress is our God,
>   A bulwark never failing;
> Our helper he, amid the flood
>   Of mortal ills prevailing.
> For still our ancient Foe
> Doth seek to work us woe;
> His craft and power are great,
> And armed with cruel hate,
> On earth is not his equal.

Satan in the Bible

Luther took "our ancient Foe" seriously, because he
is presented seriously—and extensively—in the Bible.
About a century ago, our intellectual arrogance had
reached such heights that we were ready to reject anything in the Bible that did not meet with the immediate
approval of our freshly minted scientific and historical
dogmas. Everything had to fit the measure of our minds.
Like the mythical giant, Procrustes, who stretched or com-
pressed his hapless overnight guests to fit his standard-
size bed, we manhandled and mangled the Biblical writings whenever they did not make instant "sense" in terms
of the latest Biblical scholarship.

The Bible does not respond well to such treatment. It
is too divinely resilient and self-renewing. We may take
undue liberties with God's word during carefree times—
and do so unpunished, because God is disturbingly patient. But hard times come again, and our extremity
becomes, as always, God's opportunity to reawaken us to
the full depth and majesty of his Word. It was easy to

discard the devil while Britannia ruled the waves, while our great-grandparents and grandparents were subduing a seemingly endless continent of untold wealth. Today our mood is almost chaste. Unsaved by science, dethroned from our national supremacy, half crippled by angst, we may be ready to take a new look at God's ancient Word, which has much to say about our ancient Foe.

In the Old Testament, the word "Satan" is used mostly in its literal sense of "adversary," referring to a human enemy. The earliest mention of *the* Satan as a superhuman adversary appears in the prophecy of Zechariah, where God rebukes him for accusing a faithless high priest whom God has decided to forgive (Zech. 3: 1–2).

In The Book of Job (1:6–12), Satan is given a clearly "satanic" mandate—to tempt righteous Job—but his powers are limited to carrying out God's will. He is still no enemy of God, only a malicious spirit at God's service.

The most graphic (though incognito) appearance of Satan occurs in Genesis 3. The serpent, the original tempter, is a primitive, poetic, extraordinarily vivid incarnation of Satan, of personal evil—evil so personal that it must be personified to be properly appreciated.

From these early roots, Satan blossoms forth into the superhuman Adversary of God and man whom we encounter in the Apocrypha and in the apocalyptic writings, including the book of Revelation: Here he is represented as a fallen angel who led a revolt against God and who, for that offense, was expelled from God's presence— thrown down to earth.

Jesus himself believed in the reality and the power of Satan. Whatever the physical and psychological circumstances of his temptation may have been, Jesus reported the experience as a soul-testing personal encounter with one whose stock-in-trade was corruption. At his baptism, Jesus had become aware of his mission as the suffering servant of God (Isa., ch. 53) with whom the Father would be "well pleased" (Isa. 42:1). In need of time to contemplate and confront the task God was giving him, Jesus withdrew to the desert. There Satan presented him with three time-tested ways to cut the cost, three "easy" schemes to be both Messiah and successful. (Luke 4:1–13.) What does it matter whether Jesus actually saw Satan or only heard his voice or merely felt his presence? He experienced the reality, the power of Satan more personally than most of us experience each other!

Nor can we simply write off all the exorcisms of the New Testament. Granted that psychiatry has given new names to many of the "demons" from whose tyranny Jesus freed people. There is in all mental illness a dimension of personal enslavement and a need for personal redemption to which clinical diagnosis and new and fancy names cannot do justice. After two thousand years, the grandeur of the Savior setting people free from their bondage to the Evil One is more overwhelming than ever; and we find ourselves echoing the ancient whisper: "What is this? . . . With authority he commands even the unclean spirits, and they obey him."

The Problem of Belief in Satan

It is no longer as easy as it used to be to disbelieve in Satan, but it is by no means easy to believe in him. For one thing, the very names by which he has been known in the past make it difficult for thoughtful people to believe in him. The word "devil" has been used and misused in slang, profanity, and jokes. Beelzebub and Lucifer are too literary to be suggestive. Satan is still the best name, with its primary meaning of "adversary" restored to its Biblical vigor.

A greater obstacle to belief is the memory of superstitions of bygone ages and the horrors, bigotry, and cruelty to which they had given rise. We recall from school days the story of the Salem witch trials. From the pages of medieval history, there comes to us a revolting pageant of fiends, hobgoblins, and ghosts who were only too real to simple, frightened folk. And the recent vogue of horror movies, especially those exploiting exorcism, have been compounding the difficulty. When Satan becomes good box office, the likelihood of any morally serious investigation of the Biblical image and experience of Satan is just about shot down!

A more thoughtful obstacle to belief in our ancient Foe is rooted in a mixture of poor logic and sinful pride. Logic tells us that any concession to the reality of a personal devil threatens to push us into religious dualism—into believing in two gods instead of one. The ancient religion of Persia, founded by the prophet Zoroaster, demanded belief in a good God and an equally powerful evil God. It was the responsibility of the faithful to side with the good God—and help him win.

Pride also does its part. The voice of pride tells us that, regardless of what the Bible says in its "prescientific" language, there simply cannot be any living, personal beings between God and us. This kind of pride may be on the wane today when the existence of life in "other worlds" has become a strong scientific guess, with or without "close encounters of the third kind." But it is the same kind of sinful pride that causes some of us to question the existence of God himself.

Small logic and vast pride are twin obstacles to a mature second look at Satan.

But the most deeply moral reason for refusing to believe in Satan is the fear that belief in him may tempt us to shirk our own responsibility for the evil that is so terrifyingly evident in the world. Satan, so the argument goes, is merely a projection of human evil, personified for our guilty convenience, so that our consciences may be relieved by passing the buck to him.

Who Rides the Donkey?

This argument sounds both plausible and admirable. Actually, it is neither. It is rather a case of putting the cart before the horse. It makes much more sense, in terms of what we know about ourselves, to believe that Satan is real and personal, that he works in us, enlisting us as rather willing partners in evil.

The difference—between Satan as a projection of human evil and Satan as a real partner, the *senior* partner, in human evil—may seem too subtle to be practical. But it does make all the difference in the world, *for us!* For if Satan is merely a figment of our imagination, then we are completely responsible for all the evil in ourselves and in the world at large. And if this is the case, we are helpless and damned: damned at the bar of God's justice, damned even in our own guiltily indulgent consciences. If our ancient Foe is not real, we are sunk! There is nothing for us and nothing ahead of us except more frustration, more futile remorse, more wars—until God in his mercy permits us some form of collective suicide.

There is, however, a different perspective. It is not of our invention. It offers no illusions about our ability to save ourselves. Nor does it minimize the awesome responsibility we all bear for the evil we cause, both individually and corporately. But it is a perspective that takes God's Word seriously *and offers us hope.*

Luther defined and described this Biblical perspective in his treatise on *The Bondage of the Will* in these graphic words: "The human will is like a donkey. If God mounts it, it wishes and goes as God wills. If Satan mounts it, it wishes and goes as Satan does. Nor can it choose the rider it prefers, but it is the riders who contend for its possession." (Martin Luther, *The Bondage of the Will,* tr. by Henry Cole, section XXV, p. 74; Zondervan Publishing House, 1931.)

As archaic as these words may sound, they offer the most profound, most realistic accounting of our experience of evil by affirming those Biblical insights which our own personal experience constantly confirms. What was the reaction of the disciples at that supper when Jesus announced that one of them was going to betray him? Every one of them asked, "Is it I, Lord?" They knew the evil of which they were capable. They knew that at the first sign of a real test, Satan might knock God out of the saddle to take control of their frightened, fickle wills. They knew it, and they proved it, every one of them. Not just Judas, the actual traitor, but all of them, including faithful John, who still did not manage to do more than just shuffle along, sadly, at a safe distance.

Who among us, in one of those rare, sober moments, does not realize the terrible nearness and nearly irresistible power of Satan? How many times have we gone home from church determined to make a fresh start in our marriage, in our relationship with a parent or a child, in our struggle with a habit which was getting the best of us? And how we failed—knowingly, wretchedly, listening to all the wrong and cruel words we had vowed never to speak again, slipping back into the habit which was pushing us toward a physical and moral precipice! In those moments, Satan is no theological relic, no philosophical problem, no verbal crutch. He is *real!* We feel his weight on our backs, his foul breath down our necks! And there is no self-help formula against his power. There is only outside help—help "from above."

In that wonderful passage in Ephesians 6, the author urges those new Christians to make use of the "whole armor of God," to employ all their God-given resources for the growth and strengthening of their faith, so that they might be able to "stand against the wiles of the devil" (Eph. 6:11). Then he elaborates. He speaks of "principalities and powers," of the "rulers of this present darkness" in the world, of the "spiritual hosts of wickedness in the heavenly places." Does this sound like poetry in a foreign language? Perhaps. But remember that the conflict between good and evil, which is being fought out on the battleground of your soul and mine, takes place in a cosmic setting. It is part of a battle in Satan's warfare against God. But in this warfare, according to the gospel, the conclusion is foregone and the outcome sure!

We are not Zoroastrians; we are Christians! We do not need to go to God's rescue; God has come to our rescue. Jesus of Nazareth, facing death and failure, caught a glimpse of this rescue, of God's triumph which he himself was about to secure. Beyond his cross, and beyond our crosses, Jesus glimpsed an invincible hope. And to his jittery, fingernail-biting, depressed disciples he said: "In the world you have tribulation; but be of good cheer, *I have overcome* the world." (John 16:33.)

And fifteen centuries later, in the face of all the forces Satan was mustering against him—a hostile and dangerous environment, powerful enemies, few and fickle friends, temptations of the flesh and of the heart, prospects as dim as the darkest night—Luther remembered those very words from Ephesians and all the promises of God's Word that were the lifeblood of his soul. From the depth of a fresh inkwell, he flung at our ancient Foe these lines of triumphant faith:

> Did we in our own strength confide,
>   Our striving would be losing,
> Were not the right Man on our side,
>   The Man of God's own choosing:
> Dost ask who that may be?
> Christ Jesus, it is he;
> Lord Sabaoth his name,
> From age to age the same,
> And he must win the battle.